Avril Robarts LRC

Liverpool John Moores University

KU-625-378

Department of Social Security

Research Report No. 33

Direct Payments from Income Support

Russell Mannion, Sandra Hutton and Roy Sainsbury

LIVERPOOL JMU LIBRARY

3 1111 00645 2682

London: HMSO

WITHDRAWN

© Crown copyright 1994
Applications for reproduction should be made to HMSO
First published 1994

ISBN 0 11 762290 7

Views expressed in this report may not necessarily be those of the Department or of any other Government Department.

A full list of other publications in this series is shown on page 113.

HMSO
Standing order service

Placing a standing order with HMSO BOOKS enables a
customer to receive future titles in this series automatically
as published. This saves the time, trouble and expense of
placing individual orders and avoids the problem of
knowing when to do so. For details please write to HMSO
BOOKS (PC 13A/1), Publications Centre, PO Box 276,
London SW8 5DT quoting reference 24 02 058.
The standing order service also enables customers to
receive automatically as published all material of their
choice which additionally saves extensive catalogue
research. The scope and selectivity of the service has been
extended by new techniques, and there are more than
3,500 classifications to choose from. A special leaflet
describing the service in detail may be obtained on
request.

Contents

Acknowledgements

We would like to thank all those who gave their time to be interviewed for the qualitative study and for the national survey: the Income Support recipients, third-party creditors, Benefits Agency staff and money advisers.

For other data sources and analyses we are indebted to the following:

- DSS statisticians Karen Robinson, Al Johnston and Terry Mullen from the Analytical Services Division, Newcastle upon Tyne, who prepared analyses of the Annual Statistical Enquiry on the use of direct payments and deductions.
- Richard Berthoud and Elaine Kempson at the Policy Studies Institute for making available to us the sample of Income Support recipients in their national survey of credit and debt. Julie Williams assisted in the analysis of this data.
- Maureen Astin for help with the analysis of the SPRU national survey of Income Support recipients.

Within the Department of Social Security, Dr Dan Murphy, Gillian Elam and Juliet Whitworth ensured smooth liaison with policy customers, and made possible interviews with District Office staff and the sample of recipients of Income Support. We are also very grateful to Dan Murphy for his invaluable comments on earlier drafts of the report.

Members of the project steering group were drawn from the Department of Social Security and the Benefits Agency. Wyndham Davies, John Fincham, Phil Burns, Bob Elbert and Dougie Greenshields provided valuable information about the policy context, comments and advice during the course of the research.

Within the Social Policy Research Unit we are grateful to Dr John Ditch, who supervised the research, and to Professor Sally Baldwin, Professor Gillian Parker, Dr Meg Huby, Margaret Moodie and Judith O'Leary, who were members of an internal advisery group. Thanks also to Lorna Foster who provided much-valued editorial comment on earlier versions of the report. Our special thanks go to Jenny Bowes, Sally Pulleyn and Teresa Anderson for their efficient secretarial support through the study.

The research was commissioned and funded by the Department of Social Security. The opinions expressed are those of the authors, and do not necessarily reflect the views of the Department of Social Security.

Russell Mannion
Sandra Hutton
Roy Sainsbury

Figures and Tables

Summary

Chapter One – Introduction

In 1992 the Department of Social Security commissioned the Social Policy Research Unit to undertake a study of direct payments that can be made on behalf of Income Support recipients to third-party creditors.

The aims of the research were to:

- provide an overview of the available statistical data on the numbers of recipients having direct payments and deductions as well as the number and types of direct payment and deductions

- to evaluate the usefulness of direct payments to recipients

- to examine the views and practices of third-party creditors regarding direct payments, and

- to investigate the administration of direct payments by the Benefits Agency.

Direct payments can be made for fuel, water and sewerage charges, mortgage interest and arrears, rent arrears and amenity charges, residential care and nursing home charges, hostel service charges, fines default and Community Charge/Council Tax arrears. They should be seen as a sub-set of the total deductions that can be made from benefits. The DSS also have powers to recover overpayments of benefit and repayments of loans from the Social Fund.

A number of possible advantages and disadvantages of direct payments are identified in the literature. The advantages include the perception that direct payments protect recipients from creditor sanctions, help low-income families budget by prioritising essential expenditure, spread payments throughout the year, are cheaper than many alternative methods of payment, and help those with mobility difficulties.

The possible disadvantages of direct payments identified in the literature include the criticisms that deductions from benefit may leave some recipients with an inadequate income, that the information provided by the Benefits Agency is inadequate, that direct payments are too paternalistic and reduce financial independence, and that direct payments do not provide an element of prevention against financial difficulties.

The research design comprised four main elements:

- a review of the literature and research surrounding direct payments

- interviews with Income Support recipients, Benefits Agency staff, staff of third-party creditors and money advisers. Fieldwork was conducted during the spring and summer of 1993

- a questionnaire survey of 1,137 Income Support recipients, conducted during February and March 1993

- analysis of the ASE and the PSI credit and debt survey.

Chapter Two – Use of direct payments

Between 1991 and 1993 there has been a threefold increase in the number of requests for direct payments. The main reason for this growth is the increase in requests for direct payments of Community Charge arrears. Corresponding to the growth in requests there has been a growth in the live load of direct payments cases from 486,000 in May 1991 to 1,628,000 in August 1993, a 320 per cent increase. Again payments for Community Charge arrears are a major contributory factor to this increase.

In May 1992 the most common reason for a *deduction* from Income Support was not a direct payment but for the recovery of a Social Fund loan. Social fund loans represented 39 per cent of all deductions. The next most common deduction was a direct payment for Community Charge arrears which represented 16 per cent of all deductions. Lone parents were most likely to have direct payments. Almost half of all deductions were used by lone parents, compared with 30 per cent by unemployed people and around ten per cent by disabled people and pensioners.

In May 1991 direct payments for fuel were approximately £9 per week compared with £2–4 per week for water and Community Charge. By comparison, the average deduction for the Social Fund was around £5 per week.

Geographically, most direct payments for electricity occur in two areas, those covered by Northern Electric and Yorkshire Electric. The levels of payments for electricity were highest in the South West of England. Generally the levels of all payments and deductions were higher in the London area.

In the survey of Income Support recipients over two-thirds with a deduction had a single deduction from their benefit, but more than one in ten had three or more deductions. The most common combination of two deductions was for the Social Fund and Community Charge arrears. The average number of deductions increased with the length of time a person had been on Income Support, but the average level of deductions for a given combination did not seem to rise with length of time on benefit. However, the total amount deducted did increase with the number of deductions.

Chapter Three – Coming on to direct payments

There were a number of reasons why Income Support recipients defaulted on payments to third parties. In our qualitative interviews we identified five principal causes of default. For the majority of recipients in our study, low income was an underlying factor if not always the principal reason for default. For others, a change in their circumstances, such as the breakdown of a relationship, precipitated financial difficulties. Some people attributed their arrears to their own lack of money management skills, while others reported that they withheld payments intentionally. The practices of creditors, for example underestimating current fuel consumption, was also a cause of default.

Prior to starting direct payments, people's financial situations varied widely. Some had substantial arrears to a number of third parties which had gradually increased over many months, whereas others had commenced direct payments soon after incurring sufficient arrears to qualify. People also varied in the strategies they adopted to cope with their financial situation. These strategies included doing nothing, visiting a money advice centre, and making a repayment arrangement with a creditor to clear the outstanding arrears.

For many people the transition to direct payments was a trouble-free experience. However, several reported that the length of time taken by the Benefits Agency to decide whether they were eligible for direct payments caused stress and anxiety. Others reported that third-party creditors had not been paid promptly by the Benefits Agency even though an amount had been deducted from their benefit.

Sixty-nine per cent of people in the questionnaire survey who were not currently using direct payments and who reported having budgeting difficulties, did not know about direct payments. Pensioners and disabled people were much less likely to know about the schemes than unemployed people and lone parents. Pensioners were less likely to want to use direct payments.

Although Income Support recipients may request the Benefits Agency to provide direct payments they may also be implemented without their consent. Our questionnaire survey revealed that the majority of direct payments (63 per cent) are levied rather than requested. For unemployed recipients, over 70 per cent of direct payments were levied compared with 50–60 per cent for other claimant groups. Direct payments for mortgage interest and Community Charge arrears were most likely to be levied. Direct payments for electricity and gas were levied least often.

According to Benefits Agency local office statistics, in the year to September 1993, almost a quarter (23 per cent) of requests for direct payments by benefit recipients and creditors were refused. Over twice as many requests for fuel direct payments (31 per cent) were refused, compared with requests for child support (15 per cent), rent (15 per cent) and fines (14 per cent).

Although direct payments are governed by prescribed rules and regulations, adjudication officers are still required to exercise judgment when deciding whether to accept someone on to a scheme. The most common reason for refusal was that the application was for a person not in receipt of Income Support.

Chapter Four – Experience of using direct payments

Our research shows that direct payments have a number of advantages as well as disadvantages for Income Support recipients.

Advantages

For the people in our survey and qualitative sample direct payments were effective in preventing creditor sanctions. They protected people from having fuel and water supplies disconnected, and prevented loss of homes through eviction and repossession. The schemes also helped with budgeting and prioritising payments for essential services. A quarter of people in the questionnaire survey who had direct payments for gas, water or rent felt that direct payments had made budgeting a lot easier, as did a fifth of those with a direct payment for mortgage interest. This compares with only one in ten recipients stating that direct payments for Community Charge arrears had made their budgeting a lot easier. The proportions (between a fifth and a quarter) of recipients who felt that direct payments had made budgeting worse were similar for gas, water and electricity.

Direct payments are often cheaper than alternative payment methods. Unlike prepayment meters for instance, direct payments do not incur higher tariffs. Nor are there other costs such as travel expenses. They are also a convenient method of payment for those with mobility difficulties who do not have to travel to post offices or showrooms to pay their bills.

Disadvantages

Some people in the qualitative interviews complained about the lack of information provided by the Benefits Agency and third parties about direct payments. In particular some did not know if direct payments had been made or how much of their arrears had been paid. It is currently the responsibility of third-party creditors to provide this information.

Several people had been threatened with disconnection because payments to fuel and water companies had been delayed by administrative mistakes. This caused anxiety and stress for some recipients in the study although none had actually been disconnected for this reason.

Direct payments did reduce cash flow and could make it harder to meet other household expenses. Some people in the study reported that they did not have enough to live on after direct payments had been deducted from their benefit (40 per cent in the questionnaire survey). The proportion of people reporting inadequate levels of remaining income increased with the number of direct payments they were making.

Generally, respondents reported that their fuel consumption did not increase while on direct payments. However, this was not the perception of the staff of fuel companies who reported that fuel consumption often increases while people are on direct payments. One explanation for these conflicting accounts is that current consumption may be greater than that estimated by fuel boards because the estimate is based on the consumption at the same quarter of the previous year. However, people may have been in work at that time and not needed to use so much fuel at home. Thus their current consumption may be underestimated by the fuel boards.

Direct payments do not always protect people from creditor sanctions. Although no one in the study had been subject to sanctions whilst on direct payments, money advisers reported that people having direct payments for mortgage interest are particularly vulnerable for possession proceedings if direct payments do not cover the full mortgage interest.

Chapter Five – Coming off direct payments and alternative methods of payment

A number of people in the qualitative interviews were pleased when direct payments ceased because their disposable income increased. Some also appreciated the additional choice and control that they were allowed to exercise over personal budgeting. However, others would have preferred to continue with direct payments because they helped to reduce the strain and anxiety associated with budgeting on a low income.

Some people interviewed had managed to budget successfully for household expenses after coming off direct payments. By contrast, others had experienced considerable problems and defaulted on payments. In the questionnaire survey respondents were asked how they would have managed to pay for financial commitments covered by direct payments if direct payments did not exist. The replies suggest that as many as three-quarters would have had some difficulty, at least initially, in meeting their financial commitments in the absence of direct payments.

Almost a third of people in the survey used a pre-payment meter to pay for electricity, and one in ten for gas. Pre-payment meters have a number of advantages and disadvantages for users. The advantages include removing the possibility of accruing arrears, helping to regulate fuel consumption, and allowing short-term financial flexibility. Disadvantages of pre-payment meters include the possibility of 'hidden disconnection', higher tariffs than credit meters and imposing additional costs associated with obtaining tokens and recharging keys.

Around a third of pre-payment meter users in the questionnaire survey reported that they had been subject to 'hidden disconnection' over the previous month. That is, they had wanted to use fuel on a specific occasion but had been unable to do so. The majority reported that this was due to not having enough money rather than difficulties in obtaining tokens or recharging keys.

Relatively few people paid for electricity or gas by a budget account. However, of these some found it very difficult to maintain payments for budget schemes in the face of other demands on their income.

Chapter Six – Third-party creditor perspectives

For direct payment schemes to be successful in safeguarding housing and essential utility supplies, the co-operation of third-party creditors who are paid directly is essential.

Creditors have differing attitudes and policies towards direct payments, and within the same sector local company policy can vary widely. However, all creditors, with the possible exception of some regional electricity companies, viewed direct payments as a cost-effective method of arrears recovery.

Electricity companies view pre-payment meters as more cost-effective than direct payments because they prevent the possibility of increased arrears and are economical to maintain. Technological advances in the design of pre-payment meters for water and gas may result in reducing the reliance that these sectors currently have on direct payment as a method of debt recovery.

Although creditors were generally happy with the quality of service provided by the Benefits Agency, the research did identify a range of common problems. Most creditors thought that the Benefits Agency stipulated too high an arrears figure and too long a qualifying period for direct payments to be made. In addition, they reported that they incurred additional administrative costs because of mistakes by the Benefits Agency. These usually related to incorrect identification numbers, non-payment or under- and overpayments. Many creditors were also unhappy with what they saw as variations in policy and decision making by local Benefits Agency offices.

Chapter Seven – Benefits Agency perspectives

For the most part, Benefits Agency staff thought it was in the best interests of people on Income Support to resume responsibility for current liability once arrears had been cleared. Staff also reported however that they would usually continue direct payments for specific 'vulnerable' groups. These included physically disabled people, people with learning difficulties and those who were thought to be incapable of budgeting for themselves.

Several staff thought that it would be more cost-effective to continue direct payments for people who were likely accrue further arrears and be put back on to direct payments. This would avoid the administrative cost of setting up another direct payment.

People most frequently contacted staff about problems in the initial stages of setting up a direct payment. Many of the problems associated with the processing of direct payments, particularly incorrect payments, were attributable to mistakes when transferring data between computing systems. The Benefits Agency are addressing this problem by installing integrated computer systems.

The three local Benefits Agency offices in the study generally had good working relationships with local creditors and often had joint meetings to discuss mutual problems and concerns.

Staff generally showed support for extending direct payments to non-Income Support recipients, rescheduling the current priority ordering of direct payments so that water had equal priority to fuel, and charging third parties for the service.

Chapter Eight – Policy options

Changes to the range and scope of direct payments, as well as the context within which direct payments are made, necessarily raise questions about whether and how schemes should change in response.

Our research found a great deal of support for continuing direct payments. The respondents in both the qualitative and questionnaire survey who have had experience of direct payments found them valuable in doing what they were designed to do – protect them from creditor sanctions. Creditors also said that direct payments were an effective and reliable method of debt collection. Money advisers were perhaps less enthusiastic but felt that direct payments did help people who were on Income Support who were in debt, and that therefore they should continue. Conversely, no one interviewed said that direct payments were a bad idea and should be abolished.

The response of people who use direct payments suggests that the problems identified are not so serious as to outweigh the value of the schemes. However, there are difficulties in ensuring that correct payments are made in time. Other problems exist in the estimation of current consumption for fuel, the priority of payments and the lack of knowledge about the schemes.

Administrative changes and improvements

One improvement to the current system lies in improving the information given to people about direct payments. Given the tight budgets of most people on Income

Support, there is a case for providing regular monthly statements to those on direct payments giving details of the amount being deducted from benefit, and a statement from each creditor of their account, current consumption and arrears outstanding. At present, consumers receive a quarterly account, but may build up further arrears in the interval between statements.

If monthly statements were to be sent from the DSS on deductions for direct payments, this would facilitate a more regular review of direct payment cases to check for mistakes and delays in payments. As with other options for improving the service to people on direct payments the provision of more information would inevitably increase the administrative costs of operating the schemes.

One change, the integration of the computer system, is already under way. Improved computer networks will facilitate the introduction of targets to control delays and mistakes and will enable more regular reviews of direct payment cases to be undertaken.

One way to decrease the likelihood of mistakes is to ensure that all adjudication officers, and certainly all local offices, have current copies of the guidelines and information leaflets on direct payment procedures.

A money advice service could be provided by the Benefits Agency or other established money advice agencies to people coming off direct payments. This might reduce the administration associated with starting direct payments for recipients who have come off direct payments but have again accrued arrears.

An administrative change proposed by creditors is that there should be one regional contact point in the Benefits Agency to liaise with creditors. At present some local authorities, for example, have to deal with a number of local Benefits Agency offices. This proposal might be difficult to accommodate within the present structure of the Benefits Agency based on district offices and area directorates.

There are two options for changes to the prioritisation of direct payments. First, a *pro rata* payment of debt could be used, similar to those used when an administration order is made through the courts. At present a flat rate payment of £2.20 is paid to a limited number of creditors. The benefit of a *pro rata* payment is that all eligible creditors would be entitled to payment and this might protect more people from sanctions. A problem with the *pro rata* system is that regular recalculations of payments are required. A second option is to give the user the choice of which payment they wish to make by direct payment, and which they would be prepared to make by an alternative method of payment.

In return for the security of payment of arrears by the DSS, fuel companies could be asked to monitor the consumption of those on direct payments more regularly and give monthly statements of the amount of the arrears still owing.

Structural changes

The increasing number of people using direct payments produces a corresponding rise in administrative costs. One way to contain these costs is to reduce the number and type of direct payments available. Options to do this include increasing the level of arrears which qualify for access to direct payments, or making them available only to particular categories of Income Support recipient, such as lone parents, or unemployed people with children under five. An extreme response would be to abolish direct payments altogether.

Although extreme, there are arguments for abolishing direct payments. For instance, they can be considered a legacy from more paternalistic times. The discretion allowed to adjudication officers to impose direct payments in the 'best interests of the family' take away from people the responsibility for managing their own household affairs. However, if direct payments were abolished, Income Support recipients and creditors would have to use alternative payment arrangements. There might be a consequent risk that larger numbers of people would be made homeless or disconnected from fuel or water supplies. The worst outcomes could be mitigated by curtailing the sanctions available to creditors.

The alternative to reducing or abolishing the current system of direct payments is to expand it. In our interviews, users, creditors, money advisers and even Benefits Agency staff all identified ways in which the schemes could expand. The most common suggestion was that direct payments should be available to people in receipt of other benefits and particularly to those in receipt of Invalidity Benefit. Creditors could also be required to accept a direct payment if it is agreed by the consumer and the Benefits Agency.

Other expansion measures include allowing people to continue to pay for current consumption after the arrears have been cleared, and offering direct payments as a freely available service so that recipients can use direct payments as a payment method even though they may not be in arrears. The schemes could also be expanded to cover other debts. For example, direct payments could be made to cover items such as telephone charges and television licences.

Instead of offering direct payments in specific circumstances, there may be an argument for setting up more universal banking services for low-income households. State backing is probably required to do this as private sources are unlikely to offer such a service.

There is also scope for extending the level of choice associated with direct payment schemes and reducing the discretion of adjudication officers over who is accepted and when payments are levied.

Chapter Nine – Summary and conclusion

Future policy towards direct payments will depend upon how their functions are viewed. That is, whether they perform a service of 'last resort' (the current situation) or whether they serve a wider function. The former would leave the current structure of direct payments unchanged, while the latter suggests more structural changes.

Our research has shown that abolishing the range of direct payment schemes would not benefit users nor meet with the approval of third-party creditors. The evidence that large numbers of Income Support recipients still accrue arrears for fuel, water and rent, and the increase in the types of direct payments in operation provide a strong indication that there will be a continued need for direct payments in the future.

There are a number of improvements which the Benefits Agency could make within the existing structure which would retain the underlying last resort approach.

These include providing comprehensive and regular information for people on direct payments; providing more information for potential users; providing more information on rights to appeal; and introducing targets for clearance times and performance indicators to ensure efficient processing of cases.

Other possible changes within the current structure which would enhance the preventive role of direct payments include the provision of money advice for people applying for or about to come off direct payments; reducing the qualifying times and amounts of arrears so that people can be accepted on to schemes earlier; increasing the maximum number of payments from four to five; and introducing a *pro rata* payment regime.

Third-party creditors could also contribute to improving the service to direct payment users by providing more frequent and accurate information to customers.

Although direct payments are seen as a last resort by the DSS, users also view them as a valuable aid to budgeting. This suggests a possible wider role for them. Direct payments could for instance be offered to other benefit recipients who experience difficulties with budgeting. They could also be seen as a freely available service to help people pay their bills. Direct payments could be implemented on the request of a benefit recipient rather than on an adjudication officer's decision, and extended to cover other bills such as telephone charges and television charges.

An alternative direction for policy is not to expand the services available but to restrict and target them more effectively. Options include increasing the level of arrears before a person becomes eligible for direct payments, and allowing access to prescribed groups of benefit recipients only, such as families with young children.

Another policy option to consider is charging third parties for the service. However, it would not be in the interests of Income Support recipients to pursue this policy if a likely outcome was some creditors withdrawing from the schemes or passing on the cost to their customers through higher bills.

Future policy on direct payments must not only have regard to the growth in the number and range of direct payments, but also to tensions within the present system. For example, the greater elements of compulsion in direct payments reduces the opportunity of benefit recipients to exercise financial independence and control.

In some ways these pressures and tensions are the price of success. But they also demonstrate a need for the continuation of the current direct payment schemes, at least in the medium-term, and point to an opportunity of promoting greater consumer choice and control over finances and welfare. Nevertheless, whether or not there are changes in the general policy towards direct payments, the administration of the schemes could undoubtedly be improved in the ways we have outlined to the benefit of both Income Support recipients and creditors.

Chapter 1 Introduction

For many years the DSS and previously the DHSS have deducted money from Income Support and Supplementary Benefit awards to pay directly a number of specified third-party creditors[1] on behalf of Income Support recipients.[2] These transfers of money are known as direct payments. Although their exact origins are unclear, the current range of direct payment schemes has evolved from general powers embodied in the Ministry of Social Security Act 1966, allowing the Supplementary Benefits Commission to protect the interests of a claimant or their dependants by diverting part of their benefit to 'some other person'.

The original purpose of direct payment schemes was to safeguard housing and essential utility supplies by helping benefit recipients meet their debts and pay for current consumption of fuel. More recently, they have also performed a different function by facilitating the collection of unpaid fines to magistrates' courts, Community Charge/Council Tax arrears and child maintenance.

In addition to direct payments the DSS also has powers to recover overpayments of benefit from current awards and repayments of loans from the Social Fund. Direct payments should therefore be seen as a sub-set of the total deductions that can be made from benefits and as a number of separate schemes rather than a single scheme. Direct payments can be made for fuel, water and sewerage charges, mortgage interest and arrears, rent arrears and amenity charges, residential care and nursing home charges, hostel service charges, fines default and Community Charge/Council Tax arrears. Apart from mortgage interest, they are implemented only as a service of last resort, when a recipient is in debt and where no alternative method of payment is suitable. All decisions on direct payments are made by adjudication officers.

Direct payments are of current interest for a number of reasons. In recent years there has been a substantial growth in the number of deductions from benefit and currently one in five, or just under one million, recipients are having deductions from their Income Support. The schemes have also come under the scrutiny of a number of outside organisations including the Social Security Advisery Committee, the Public Utilities Access Forum and the National Association of Citizens Advice Bureaux (NACAB), who have all published reports in the last four years about the practical operation of, and the principles underlying, direct payment schemes.

These bodies generally support the use of direct payments and identify a number of advantages of the schemes. First, it is thought direct payments protect Income Support recipients from creditor sanctions, are effective in safeguarding essential utility supplies (gas, electricity and water) and in preventing the loss of a claimant's home through eviction or repossession. Secondly, it is believed that they help low-income families to manage their finances by prioritising essential expenditure and spreading payments evenly through the year. Thirdly, direct payments are cheaper than many alternative methods of payment, particularly pre-payment meters, and perform a similar service as a direct debit or standing order for those without a bank or building society account. Finally, because creditors are paid directly, they can help people who experience problems travelling to post offices, banks or showrooms to pay bills.

In contrast to these advantages, some problems with the schemes are reported. First, concern has been expressed that deductions from benefit, and in particular multiple

---

1 Third-party creditors include mortgage lenders, local authorities, fuel and water companies.

2 To avoid confusion with the customers of third-party creditors we use the term recipient to describe individuals receiving Income Support.

deductions can leave some Income Support recipients with an inadequate income to live on. Secondly, criticism has been made that the information provided to people by creditors and the Benefits Agency is inadequate, particularly concerning the availability and operation of the schemes. Thirdly, some bodies such as NACAB view direct payment schemes as being intrinsically paternalistic and criticise the level of choice afforded to recipients. Specifically, concern has been expressed about the discretion that adjudication officers have over levying and determining access to direct payments. Finally, because direct payments are a service of 'last resort', their capacity for helping benefit recipients is limited. In particular they do not anticipate or help to prevent financial difficulties.

Against this background of interest and concern the Department of Social Security commissioned the Social Policy Research Unit to undertake a study of the operation of direct payment schemes. The aims of the research were:

- to provide an overview of the available statistical data on the following:
    - numbers of Income Support recipients having direct payments and deductions
    - numbers and types of direct payments and deductions
    - numbers and types of multiple direct payments and deductions
    - level of direct payments and deductions
    - duration of direct payments and deductions

- to evaluate the usefulness of direct payment schemes to recipients. In particular we were requested to investigate the range of factors that contribute to the need for direct payments; the effect of direct payments on recipients' capacity to budget; the needs unmet by current schemes; the capacity of existing priorities to protect the interests of recipients; the consequences for recipients who are refused direct payments; and the consequences of coming off direct payments

- to examine the views and practices of third-party creditors regarding direct payments and assess the financial and social welfare implications of the alternative payment methods available to low-income groups

- to investigate the administration of direct payment schemes by the Benefits Agency and in particular explore the criteria used by staff when adjudicating direct payment decisions.

The fieldwork for the research and the national survey of Income Support recipients were both carried out in the spring and summer of 1993.

The legislative basis for deductions from benefit

No single set of regulations governs all forms of deduction from benefit. The deductions made to pay third parties (as opposed to repaying the Secretary of State) are mainly contained in Schedules 9 and 9A to the Social Security (Claims and Payments) Regulations 1987 under the powers contained in Section 5(1)(p) of the Social Security Administration Act 1992. Those not included in these regulations are as follows:

- Community Charge: Sections 22(3) and 146(6) of, and paragraph 6 of Schedule 4 to, the Local Government Finance Act 1988. The Community Charges (Deductions from Income Support) (Scotland) Regulations 1989, and the Community Charges (Deductions from Income Support) (No. 2) Regulations 1990

- Council Tax: Sections 14(3), 97(5), 113 and 116(1) of, paragraphs 1 and 6 of Schedule 4 and paragraph 6 of Schedule 8 to, the Local Government Finance Act 1992. The Council Tax (Deductions from Income Support) Regulations 1993

- Fines: Sections 24 and 30 of the Criminal Justice Act 1991, and the Fines (Deductions from Income Support) Regulations 1992.

The structure of direct payment schemes

Direct payments are made subject to the following circumstances:

Rent arrears (inclusive of water, and fuel charges): If an Income Support recipient is in arrears to a landlord a sum of money can be deducted from benefit and paid direct to the landlord. The amount in arrears must be equivalent to four times the weekly rent and accrued over at least eight weeks. It is also necessary for the landlord to request such a direct payment arrangement. However, deductions can be made if the debt has accrued over less than eight weeks if an adjudication officer decides it is in the 'overriding interests of the family'.

Mortgage interest (and other housing costs): Direct payments can be made for arrears and to meet current costs of mortgage interest. Since May 1992, most Income Support recipients with a mortgage have had payment of their mortgage interest made directly by the Benefits Agency to the lender after the first 16 weeks. Direct payments can be made for mortgage interest arrears before 16 weeks if it is in the interest of the family and if less than eight weeks' payments have been made in the previous 12 weeks. For other housing costs, the debt must exceed half the annual total of the relevant housing cost, unless there is an overriding interest of the claimant that direct payment should start immediately.

Fuel debts (gas and electricity): Direct payments can be made for fuel where the amount of debt exceeds £44 (including reconnection charges if already disconnected) and where an adjudication officer decides that it is in the interests of the family. The amount deducted for current consumption is whatever is necessary to meet requirements. A deduction in respect of current consumption may continue after a debt has been cleared.

Water and sewerage charges: Direct payments can be made if there is a debt and it is in the interests of the family, although no minimum amount of arrears is specified. Because water companies bill customers in advance (six or 12 months), a charge for current consumption is interpreted as a debt if it is not paid by the due date.

Arrears for Community Charge and Council Tax: Direct payments can be made from Income Support if the local authority has obtained a liability order from a magistrates' court (in Scotland, a summary warrant or a decree from a Sheriff's court). A direct payment for Council Tax arrears cannot be made if direct payments are already being made for Community Charge arrears or vice versa.

Other accommodation and service charges: Direct payments can be made to cover various service charges and payments required of people living in residential and nursing homes, hostels and Part III accommodation. With certain exceptions (for example accommodation for alcoholics and drug addicts) direct payments will only be made if an adjudication officer decides it is in the interests of the family.

Child support maintenance: In certain cases, if the claimant is an absent parent, deductions may be made at the request of a Child Support Officer for payment to the person with care of the child.

Fines: Direct payments may be made where a claimant aged 18 or over defaults on paying a fine or compensation order and the magistrates' court has held a means enquiry.

Direct payments can only be made if a person is in receipt of Income Support. However, direct payments can be made from persons receiving other benefits if that benefit is combined with Income Support in the same order book or giro cheque. This does not apply for Community Charge arrears and Council Tax arrears where sums can be paid from Income Support only.

Level of direct payments

Direct payments can be made for current liability (*estimated* in the case of metered fuel or water charges, or *actual* in the case of service charges paid with rent, residential care and nursing home charges, mortgage interest and non-metered water charges) as well as for arrears.

There is no provision for deductions for hostel service charge debts as these charges can be paid direct from the outset of the stay at the hostel. There cannot be deductions for current rent as these are covered by Housing Benefit. When the debt is cleared, deductions for current consumption may only continue if it is in the 'interests of the family'.

Standard deductions for debts

Direct payments for debts for housing, utilities, Community Charge, fines, Council Tax and child maintenance are at the fixed rate of five per cent of the Income Support personal allowance for a single person aged 25 or over (£2.20 a week from April 1993). The exception to this is where a court order has been obtained against a couple for Community Charge arrears, where the deduction is at five per cent of the standard Income Support personal allowance for a couple (£3.45 a week from April 1993).

Ceilings on deductions

There is an overall limit of three times five per cent of the single over 25 personal allowance (£6.60) for the recovery of debts, so normally only three debts can be paid in this way.

Exceptions to this are:

- deductions for Community Charge arrears may be made on top of the 'three times five per cent' ceiling

- current fuel and water charges have no limit on the amount that can be deducted from benefit

- Social Fund loans may normally be recovered at a rate not exceeding 15 per cent of the *total Income Support entitlement – or 'applicable amount'* – for the claimant and family, *less* any housing costs included in Income Support, and may be reduced to take account of higher priority deductions. The rate of recovery may exceed this level with the consent of the applicant, but only up to a rate of 25 per cent

- recoveries of overpayments are normally made up to a maximum of 'three times five per cent' of benefit. If the recipient has earnings or income subject to the £5 or £15 disregard, the deduction may be increased by half this amount

- overpayment recovery may be made up to a maximum of 'four times five per cent' of benefit, where there has been a successful prosecution for fraud or the claimant has admitted fraud

- deductions for mortgage interest are not included in the limit as extra Income Support is awarded to pay for this.

Deductions for direct payments for housing (except under the new compulsory mortgage direct payment scheme), fuel and water are normally made with the claimant's consent, although this is not necessary. Consent must be obtained, however, if the total deduction for arrears and current charges of fuel, water and service charges, plus arrears of housing costs, exceeds 25 per cent of a family's total Income Support applicable amount, less housing costs.

Exceptions to this are:

- direct payments for Income Support housing costs ineligible for Housing Benefit. This is because specific provision is made in the Income Support payment for such housing costs as mortgage interest

- deductions in respect of Community Charge arrears, child maintenance, unpaid fines and Council Tax arrears.

There is a statutory order of priority for all deductions which include Social Fund loans and overpayments. No more than three deductions for arrears (as opposed to current consumption only where arrears have been cleared) can be made. The order of priority is as follows:

1st   Housing costs (within these mortgage payments have highest priority)

2nd   Rent arrears (and related charges)

3rd   Fuel charges (priority between gas and electricity determined by the adjudication officer according to circumstances)

4th   Water and sewerage charges

5th   Community Charge and Council Tax arrears

6th   Fines

7th   Child maintenance

8th   Social Fund

9th   Overpayments.

Research design and methods

Each of the participants involved with direct payment schemes could have differing views about the usefulness and effectiveness of direct payment schemes. We therefore decided to adopt a pluralistic research design which allowed a number of perspectives to be included in the evaluation of direct payments. We used both quantitative and qualitative research methods, where appropriate, to analyse the number and characteristics of Income Support recipients on direct payments and to explore the processes associated with the schemes.

The research design comprised four main elements:

- *A review of the literature and research* surrounding direct payments. This review covered the literature on money management and styles of budgeting; research on credit and debt; and statistics of third-party arrears and sanctions

- *In-depth interviews* were conducted in three areas of the country. In each of these areas, interviews were conducted with Income Support recipients, Benefits Agency staff, third-party creditors and staff from local advice services. A number of third parties were also contacted by telephone for their views about direct payments. Appendix One contains details of the research design and methodology for this part of the study. The topic guides used for the in-depth interviews are reproduced in Appendix Two

- *A questionnaire survey* of Income Support recipients was used to obtain the views and experiences of recipients regarding direct payments. We added questions to a national survey of Income Support recipients concerned with changing circumstances. Interviews were conducted with 1,137 Income Support recipients during February and March 1993. Of these people, 309 currently had direct payments or had had them within the previous six months. Details of the survey methods can be found in Appendix Three, and the specific questions concerning direct payments are contained in Appendices Four and Five

- *The Annual Statistical Enquiry* (ASE) was used to compare the use of direct payments by different types of recipient, regional variation in the use of direct payments, levels of deductions, and combinations of deduction. See Appendix Three for a discussion of the ASE.

Structure of the report

In writing this report we have drawn upon all the sources of data relevant for each chapter. In consequence we have merged both quantitative and qualitative information where appropriate rather than present each set of data separately.

Chapter Two sets the context for later chapters by presenting an analysis of data from the ASE and our national survey of benefit recipients on the scope of the direct payment schemes. Chapter Three explores the circumstances of recipients prior to using direct payments, their experiences in applying for one of the schemes, and examines why some recipients are refused. In Chapter Four we examine the general usefulness of direct payments by analysing their advantages and disadvantages as reported by recipients themselves. Chapter Five explores the experience of recipients who come off direct payments and discusses the issues surrounding the use of alternatives. Chapter Six presents the views of third-party creditors about the direct payment schemes and examines their practices. Chapter Seven explores the experiences, perceptions and opinions of Benefits Agency staff who are routinely involved with the day-to-day administration of direct payments. Chapter Eight presents a number of policy options arising from our study and the final chapter provides a summary and conclusion to the research.

Methodological note on the use of qualitative data

As part of our study we interviewed 45 Income Support recipients about direct payments. Since our sample was not intended to be statistically representative of the general population of Income Support recipients, findings outlined in the report based on these interviews cannot be generalised in a quantitative manner. Our analysis provides illustrations and explanations, and explores patterns among a small sample group. Numbers are occasionally used for purposes of description, but give no indication about representation in the general population. When very strong patterns emerge, for example where the majority of recipients describe a similar experience, then attention will be drawn to this. In the same light, single exceptions or particularly unusual circumstances can provide valuable insights and new perspectives, so these are also mentioned when they occur. Throughout the report, verbatim quotations from the interviews are used to illustrate specific themes and issues.

In contrast to the qualitative sample, the samples for the ASE and our own survey are representative of Income Support recipients. Findings from these two sources can therefore be generalised.

Chapter 2   Use of Direct Payments

This chapter, based mainly on analysis of DSS administrative statistics, gives an overview of the numbers and types of direct payments in operation, and how they are used by different claimant groups.

The first section describes the full range of data used. As the analysis is rather concentrated, the second section outlines the main results before the sections containing the detailed analyses. Analyses cover both direct payments and other deductions from Income Support. The analysis is presented in sections three to six. Section three considers the growth in the numbers of direct payments in operation; the fourth section investigates whether some types of people on Income Support use them more than others, and whether this depends upon the area they live in. The combinations of direct payments which occur most often and the relationship between combinations, level of deductions and time on benefit is investigated in section five. The sixth section outlines the use of direct payments by respondents to the national survey of recipients of Income Support and compares this with information from administrative statistics.

Data used

Most of the analyses presented in this chapter are from the Annual Statistical Enquiry (ASE). The other main source of information was the national survey of recipients of Income Support which included specific questions on the use of direct payments. We also investigated two further data sources: the Family Expenditure Survey (FES), and a recent national survey by the Policy Studies Institute (PSI) of experience of credit and debt (Berthoud and Kempson, 1992). Details of these data sources are given in Appendix Three.

The ASE gathers information on a one per cent sample of recipients of Income Support in May each year. Detailed analyses have been made available by DSS statisticians at the request of the researchers. Most of the analyses presented here refer to the ASE for May 1991, but some of the main tables were repeated and updated using information for May 1992.

The FES proved to be unsuitable for our purposes because the most relevant question, about whether direct payments are used in paying for fuel has been discontinued since 1988. Considerable changes to the direct payment schemes have taken place since then so the value of any analysis of the 1988 FES as a guide to current use is questionable. Although the 1991 FES included a question on whether any items of household expenditure had been paid directly by someone outside the household, it is not clear that direct payments by the DSS would be easily identified. Nor is it obvious how such an analysis would add to the information we have from the national sample of Income Support recipients.

The PSI study undertaken in 1989 is a rich source of information on financial management, but the number with direct payments is relatively small, only 62. Although the direct payment schemes have changed substantially since 1989, the additional information on attitudes to debt was worth exploring and are set out in Appendix Six.

Summary of main results

This chapter is mainly concerned with setting the context for the study. The growth in the numbers and types of direct payments raises questions about the costs of administration of these proliferating schemes and about the consequences for those on Income Support of increasing numbers of deductions. As will be seen in subsequent chapters, one of the areas investigated in this research is the value and usefulness of direct payments to recipients of Income Support and to creditors. If they are useful then growth might not be a problem.

Between 1991 and 1992, there was a threefold increase in the number of requests for direct payments. The main reason for this growth was the increase in requests for the direct payment of Community Charge arrears. However, the change from the Community Charge to the Council Tax might mean that this is a bulge which will dissipate as Community Charge arrears work their way through the system. Corresponding to the growth in requests has been a growth in the number of direct payments made; the proportion of requests accepted has changed little.

The most common reason for a deduction from Income Support was for the recovery of a Social Fund loan – 39 per cent of all deductions in May 1992. The next most common was a direct payment for Community Charge arrears (16 per cent) and to gas companies (13 per cent). In general the schemes were mainly used by lone parents and unemployed people rather than disabled people and pensioners. Almost half of all deductions were used by lone parents, compared with around ten per cent by disabled people and pensioners, and 30 per cent by unemployed recipients.

Direct payments for fuel were around £9 per week compared with £2–4 per week for water, Community Charge and overpayments. The average deduction for the Social Fund was around £5 per week. Payments for mortgage interest were much larger, but they are a transfer payment rather than a deduction from benefit.

Geographically, most payments for electricity occurred in the areas covered by Northern Electric, Yorkshire Electric and in Scotland. The level of direct payments for electricity was highest in the South West, a rural area with a relatively high proportion of households with no mains gas. Generally the levels of all payments and deductions were higher in the London area.

Overall around a fifth of all those on Income Support had a deduction from benefit. Some people had direct payments and deductions for more than one item and we investigated the combinations of deductions which occurred together. Most of those with deductions (67 per cent) had only one deduction, but 12 per cent had three or more. Of those with any deductions, over a third had a single deduction for the Social Fund, and the next most common was one deduction for Community Charge arrears (11 per cent). The most common combination of two deductions was for the Social Fund and the Community Charge used by four per cent of those with deductions. Deductions for gas, electricity and the Social Fund were the most common combination of three deductions.

The number of deductions increased with the length of time on Income Support, but the level of deductions for a given combination did not seem to rise with time on benefit. However, if the number of deductions rises, the overall level of deduction is likely to increase. With two deductions the amount of benefit deducted varied from £9.11 for rent and Social Fund deductions to £16.14 for electricity and Social Fund deductions. The most common of three deductions, for electricity, gas and the Social Fund resulted in an average deduction of £21.06.

Information gathered from the national survey of Income Support recipients in early 1993 was compared with the analysis of the ASE on the proportions of different types of direct payments and the distribution of numbers of direct payments. The sample in our survey corresponded well to the ASE and this provides a sound basis for the more detailed analyses of the survey information later in the report.

Growth in the use of direct payments

As shown in Table 2.1 there was nearly a 300 per cent growth in the requests for direct payments between March 1991 and September 1993 from 47,000 to 136,000. Not all of these will have been requests from people on Income Support, but will also have come from creditors and money advisers and are best thought of as requests to start a direct payment. Although the overall trend in requests for direct payments was upwards, there were variations. Requests noticeably fell in August and December, the main holiday months. Surprisingly there were fewer requests in April and May 1993 than the trend would suggest, and it is not clear why this occurred.

Table 2.1 Requests for direct payments[1]

Month	Number of requests in '000s	Month	Number of requests in '000s	Month	Number of requests in '000s
1991		**1992**		**1993**	
		January	114	January	140
		February	163	February	141
March	47	March	–	March	134
April	49	April	102	April	95
May	53	May	103	May	97
June	56	June	119	June	125
July	68	July	116	July	132
August	67	August	106	August	130
September	74	September	115	September	136
October	79	October	113		
November	77	November	125		
December	56				

[1] This table is compiled from two series, March 1991 to February 1992 and April 1992 to September 1993.
Source: Benefits Agency local office statistics; subject to revisions

Not all requests for direct payments are accepted by the adjudication officer, for example the amount of arrears must be over a certain level and benefit must be sufficient to make the payment. Table 2.2 below shows the proportions of requests actually accepted.

Table 2.2 Percentage of direct payment requests accepted

	Percentage accepted		Number of requests	
	March 1991	**February 1992**	**March 1991**	**February 1992**
Fuel	64	66	20,600	27,800
Rent	74	81	7,400	11,800
Water	74	86	7,600	14,700
Community Charge	83	78	10,000	64,300
Other	79	49	1,600	44,700[1]

[1] This figure seems very large. It could be due to new requests for direct payments which have not yet been classified. The Benefits Agency tables from which it is taken are subject to revisions.
Source: Benefits Agency local office statistics

Acceptance of requests for direct payments varied from 86 per cent for water charges to 66 per cent for fuel and 49 per cent for 'other' payments. The table shows that the proportion of requests accepted for payments for fuel direct have remained much the same at around two-thirds from March 1991 to February 1992. This could be because direct payments for fuel have been part of the system for a long time and the process has stabilised; creditors and administrators are more familiar with the rules. In contrast, direct payments for water charges are relatively recent, and the proportion of requests accepted has risen from 74 per cent to 86 per cent. Payments for the Community Charge are also relatively new and the proportion of requests accepted has fallen from 83 per cent to 78 per cent. The fall in the proportion accepted for other direct payments could also be because of changes to the system. The 'other' category includes those with more than one direct payment of a similar type, and deductions for residential or nursing home care. If a direct payment is allowed in new circumstances, in some offices it is categorised a payment for 'other' items until a separate category is established. The rise in the proportion accepted for payment of rent arrears cannot be attributed to payments for rent arrears being new to the system. Direct payments for rent arrears have a long history, and it is not clear why there should be such fluctuation.

Alternatively, a degree of change might be part of normal fluctuation, and the stability of the fuel direct figures is simply a result of having only two data points to compare.

It is important to monitor the proportion of requests for direct payments which are accepted in each office. If the proportion of acceptances to requests is low, then information about the system could be inadequate or misinterpreted by possible users, creditors and other agencies, or even by the local office. Both of these have administrative costs: the first the cost of processing unnecessary requests; and the second the cost of possible appeals. A high proportion of acceptances might indicate that local office staff are wrongly allowing some direct payments.

Table 2.2 also shows the change in numbers of requests for direct payments over the year from March 1991 to February 1992. One of the most striking results from the analysis of the data on requests from direct payments is the substantial growth over this period, and this seems to be in large part due to the growth in requests for payments for Community Charge arrears. The numbers of requests for direct payments for Community Charge arrears rose from 10,002 to 64,344 requests over the year, an increase of 643 per cent. In March 1991 the most common request for direct payments was for fuel, but a year later it was for the Community Charge and for 'other' payments. Table 2.2 also shows that the numbers of requests for other direct payments have grown over the year from March 1991 to February 1992. The numbers of requests for direct payment for fuel and rent have grown least, but requests for payments for water charges have almost doubled.

As Table 2.3 shows, corresponding to the growth in requests, the number of direct payments rose by 320 per cent from 486,000 to 1,628,000 from May 1991 to August 1993. The main contributors to this rise were Community Charge and mortgage interest payments. The relative proportions of different types of payment have also changed. Fuel payments were 52 per cent of all direct payments in May 1991, but by August 1993 they had fallen to 20 per cent. In contrast, payments for the Community Charge were 12 per cent of all payments in May 1991 and 34 per cent by August 1993, and mortgage interest payments have risen from two to 23 per cent. The proportions of other payments have remained similar over time: water charges fluctuating between 13 per cent and 17 per cent; residential care and nursing homes, hostels and night shelter charges remaining under one per cent.

Table 2.3 Growth in the number of direct payments, May 1991 to August 1993[1]

	Numbers of direct payments, '000s							
	May 1991		August 1991		August 1992		August 1993	
	N	%	N	%	N	%	N	%
Fuel	254	52	262	47	306	34	318	20
Rent arrears/amenity charges	91	19	100	18	136	15	162	10
Water charges	69	14	84	15	147	17	206	13
Community Charge	58	12	90	16	260	29	555	34
Mortgage interest	8	2	9	2	31	3	371	23
Residential care/nursing home	4	1	4	1	4	<1	4	<1
Hostel/night shelter charges	2	<1	3	1	3	<1	4	<1
Community care	–	–	–	–	–	–	2	<1
Council Tax	–	–	–	–	–	–	<1	–
Child support	–	–	–	–	–	–	2	<1
Unpaid fines	–	–	–	–	–	–	4	<1
All	**486**	**100**	**553**	**100**	**887**	**100**	**1,628**	**100**

[1] A significant number of Income Support recipients have more than one deduction.
Source: Benefits Agency statistics

Information on current use of different types of direct payment, including other deductions, is set out in Table 2.4. This table also includes information on other deductions from benefit for recovery of overpayments and Social Fund loans.

Table 2.4 Numbers of Income Support recipients with deductions, May 1992

Deduction	Number of recipients	Per cent of all deductions	Per cent of all recipients of IS
Electricity	95,000	6	1.9
Gas	192,000	13	3.8
Rent arrears/amenity	85,000	6	1.7
Water charges	132,000	9	2.6
Community Charge	243,000	16	4.8
Mortgage interest	44,000	3	0.9
Other housing costs	14,000	1	0.3
Residential care/nursing home fees	1,000	<1	<0.1
Part III and Polish homes	0	0	0.0
Hostel charges	1,000	<1	<0.1
Unpaid fines recovery	0	0	0.0
Social Fund recovery	586,000	39	11.5
Overpayments recovery	92,000	6	1.8

Source: ASE, May 1992

The most common reason for a deduction from benefit is to repay a Social Fund loan, followed by direct payments to cover Community Charge arrears. Thus recoveries of Social Fund loans are 39 per cent of all deductions from benefit (586,000 cases), repayments of Community Charge arrears, 16 per cent (243,000 cases); repayments of arrears and current consumption of gas are 13 per cent (192,000 cases); and water charges, nine per cent (132,000 cases). The growth in the numbers using direct payments and in the number of reasons for deductions from benefit highlights the changing role and function of direct payments since the early days of fuel and rent direct.

Those who use direct payments, however, are still a minority of those on Income Support. The final column in Table 2.4 shows the percentage of all those on Income Support who have each kind of deduction from benefit. Except for the Social Fund, fewer than five per cent of those on Income Support have any specific deduction; for example, 4.8 per cent have a direct payment for Community Charge arrears, 3.8 per cent for gas and 2.6 per cent for water. In contrast, 11.5 per cent are paying back a Social Fund loan.

Use of direct payments by different groups of claimants

Table 2.5 shows that lone parents and unemployed claimants are much more likely to have a direct deduction from benefit than pensioners and sick or disabled people. Lone parents accounted for nearly half of all deductions (48 per cent) followed by unemployed people who accounted for nearly a third (30 per cent) whereas disabled people accounted for 10 per cent and pensioners and others only 12 per cent.

The use of particular direct payments varies with the category of Income Support claimant. Disabled people are more likely to have payments for gas, electricity and overpayments than average, whereas lone parents are even more likely to have payments for gas but not overpayments. Unemployed claimants have a lower proportion of payments for fuel but more for the Social Fund than average. Because so few pensioners use direct deductions they have been included with other claimants, and this combined group is more likely than average to pay rent direct and to have deductions for overpayments.

Table 2.5   Use of deductions by type of deduction and recipient type

Deduction	All cases	Disabled	Lone parent	Unemployed	Any other category
	%	%	%	%	%
Electricity	10.0	14.2	10.6	7.4	10.4
Gas	15.2	16.7	18.2	10.5	13.6
Rent and amenity	9.8	9.3	9.4	9.8	11.5
Water	7.0	7.4	7.1	6.2	7.8
Community Charge	3.5	3.4	2.4	4.7	5.0
Mortgage interest	0.7	0.6	0.8	0.5	1.2
Overpayment	7.1	8.4	5.4	8.3	9.5
Social Fund	46.1	39.6	45.7	51.8	39.2
All others	0.7	0.4	0.6	0.6	1.9
Total deductions	**960,500**	**95,400**	**463,800**	**284,100**	**117,200**
Percentage by claimant types	**100**	**10**	**48**	**30**	**12**

Source: Table 10.1 Income Support Statistics Annual Enquiry, May 1991

Table 2.6 shows the level of deduction for the main types of deduction and claimant groups.

Table 2.6   Level of deductions by type of deduction and recipient type

Deduction	All cases	Disabled	Lone parent	Unemployed	Any other category
	£ per week	£ per week	£ per week	£ per week	£ per week
Electricity	9.86	9.19	10.14	9.85	9.50
Gas	9.31	8.41	9.71	9.14	8.43
Rent and amenity	3.81	4.59	3.74	3.53	4.11
Water	4.55	4.49	4.62	4.54	4.35
Community Charge	2.08	2.03	2.10	2.05	2.12
Mortgage interest	40.04	42.75	44.60	41.26	26.18
Overpayment	3.68	4.27	3.37	3.67	3.97
Social Fund	5.53	5.48	5.87	5.13	5.30
All others	29.91	7.82	6.50	17.98	71.34
Total deductions	**960,500**	**95,400**	**463,800**	**284,100**	**117,200**
Percentage by claimant types	**100**	**10**	**48**	**30**	**12**

Source: Analysis of Income Support Statistics Annual Enquiry, May 1991

As Table 2.6 shows, lone parents have higher deductions for both gas and electricity than other groups. The level of deduction for fuel reflects current consumption in addition to repayment of arrears though it is not possible to say which contributes more. It is probably a combination of both for two reasons. First, families are more likely to be in debt than pensioners, and, secondly, demand for fuel depends on the number of people in the household, and the households of lone parents are likely to be larger than those of pensioners and disabled people (Hutton, 1984). The household sizes of unemployed claimants are more varied, but many of the unemployed will consist of single young people and people made redundant late in their working life, and these smaller households will bring the average consumption down. There are relatively few men with wives and families in receipt of Income Support. Only 13 per cent of those on Income Support live with partners and are under pension age, and not all of these will have children (Social Security Statistics, 1992).

Lone parents are also likely to have higher deductions for the Social Fund and for water charges than others. They also differ from others in that fewer make repayments for the recovery of overpayments (Table 2.5) and when they do, they have a lower level of deduction. This is interesting since other work shows that lone parents are more likely than others to experience changes in circumstances and have more frequent contact with the Benefits Agency (Sainsbury, Hutton and Ditch, 1994). Hence, Income Support awards to lone parents are likely to be reviewed more frequently than for other recipient groups. This reduces the possibility of an incorrect award which might generate an overpayment. Also, more frequent reviews will mean that any overpayments that do arise are identified relatively quickly, thus reducing the amount of benefit that has to be repaid.

Direct payments for mortgage interest are included in these tables because they are administered by the direct payments section of local offices, but they are different in nature from other payments. They are a transfer payment similar to Housing Benefit for tenants and are generally for larger amounts than other direct payments. Because of the size of the payments, any failure in the liaison between all the parties involved could quickly lead to serious difficulty (see Chapter Four).

Table 2.7 shows that 29 per cent of all deductions are accounted for by lone parents with children under five, compared with 20 per cent by lone parents with children over five. Lone parents with children under five have little opportunity to supplement Income Support with earnings, despite the disregard, because of the cost and scarcity of child-care facilities (Bradshaw and Millar, 1991). Also the type of deduction differs between the two groups of lone parents. Those with children under five are more likely to have deductions for a Social Fund loan, whereas those with children over five are more likely to use direct payments for electricity, gas, and water. Lone parents with children over five are likely to be older and separated or divorced (Haskey, 1989). They may remain in the family home and have less need of major household items whereas those with children under five are likely to be younger; some will be single mothers setting up home for the first time. Couples, whether or not with children under five, make relatively little use of direct payments or deductions. Pensioners use them even less.

One group with a surprising number of deductions from benefit is single men aged under 60. A small number will be single fathers, but the majority will be single, unemployed men. Some men on their own as a result of relationship breakdown will have had to set up an independent home so they may have a relatively high use of Social Fund loans. Apart from this group, single unemployed men tend to be young and still in the process of acquiring household goods.

Some further differences between groups are revealed in the analysis of levels of deduction by family type shown in Table 2.8. Although lone parents are more likely to have deductions for the Social Fund, couples have higher levels of deductions. In contrast, the level of direct payment to the utilities are similar for lone parents and couples. The income of couples is greater than that of lone parents so the amount left for other expenses will be lower for lone parents than couples. The 'All others' category includes direct payments for other accommodation and service charges; for unpaid fines; and for residential care and nursing home accommodation. Men and women over 60 seem to have high levels of direct payment, and it seems likely that many of these are for nursing or residential care.

In general, pensioners and single men have lower levels of deductions than families with children.

Table 2.7 Use of deductions by type of deduction and family type

Deduction	All cases	Lone parent, child under 5	Lone parent, none under 5	Couple, child under 5	Couple, children none under 5	Man, under 60†	Woman, under 60	Man, 60 and over	Woman, 60 and over	Couple, 60 and over
	%	%	%	%	%	%	%	%	%	%
Electricity	10.0	9.6	12.2	7.5	13.1	6.2	10.7	16.0	12.7	14.0
Gas	15.2	16.8	20.3	16.5	16.8	7.3	12.5	10.7	18.7	15.2
Rent and amenity	9.8	8.0	10.9	8.1	10.1	10.0	11.9	15.3	12.4	11.1
Water	7.0	6.6	9.1	8.1	7.6	4.8	4.9	14.5	9.4	7.6
Community Charge	3.5	2.3	2.5	3.2	2.8	5.5	6.9	3.1	4.9	3.5
Mortgage interest	0.7	0.6	1.1	0.8	1.1	0.3	0.2	0.8	1.9	1.8
Overpayment	7.1	4.8	6.3	7.7	11.7	7.5	7.7	11.5	9.4	14.0
Social Fund	46.1	50.8	38.0	47.6	36.2	56.8	44.6	26.0	30.0	32.7
All others	0.7	0.6	0.6	0.6	0.5	1.5	0.8	2.3	0.7	–
Total deductions	960,500	282,300	193,900	93,100	63,200	171,400	66,600	13,100	26,700	17,100
Percentage by claimant types	100	29.4	20.2	9.7	6.6	17.8	6.9	1.4	2.8	1.8

† Includes single fathers
Source: Analysis of Income Support Statistics Annual Enquiry, May 1991

Table 2.8 Level of deductions by type of deduction and family type

Deduction	All cases	Lone parent, child under 5	Lone parent, none under 5	Couple, child under 5	Couple, children none under 5	Man, under 60†	Woman, under 60	Man, 60 and over	Woman, 60 and over	Couple, 60 and over
	£ per week	£ per week	£ per week	£ per week	£ per week	£ per week	£ per week	£ per week	£ per week	£ per week
Electricity	9.86	10.15	10.26	10.35	11.16	8.84	6.53	7.69	9.24	9.82
Gas	9.31	9.60	9.77	9.78	9.91	7.81	7.13	8.48	7.39	9.45
Rent and amenity	3.81	3.57	3.49	3.46	4.57	3.97	3.36	3.61	3.92	5.32
Water	4.55	4.53	4.73	4.88	4.53	4.19	3.96	4.33	4.05	4.84
Community Charge	2.08	2.03	2.19	2.21	2.13	1.99	1.96	2.00	2.11	2.84
Mortgage interest	40.04	45.47	45.96	38.21	39.41	42.17	20.06	7.65	25.41	12.13
Overpayment	3.68	2.82	3.98	2.73	4.50	4.00	3.56	4.10	3.81	5.19
Social Fund	5.53	5.97	5.67	7.16	7.09	4.46	3.31	5.52	4.31	6.95
All others	29.91	5.00	8.90	3.57	4.03	51.40	43.20	47.41	99.99	0

† Includes single fathers
Source: Analysis of Income Support Annual Enquiry, 1991

14

Regional variation in the use of direct payments

Different parts of the country are served by different utility companies, local authorities, building societies and others involved in direct payments from benefit. This analysis investigates whether particular types of direct payment are more likely in some parts of the country than others. The information presented here is further supplemented in Chapter Six on the use of direct payments by third-party creditors. In considering geographical variation, we used electricity board areas rather than standard regions although they are to some extent contiguous. It seemed likely that there would be variation between electricity companies in their use of direct payments as some were actively promoting the use of pre-payment meters as an alternative to direct payments. Use of standard regions might blur any differences. Similar analyses could be done for gas regions, but they are very large and do not seem to have differing policies. Nor did it seem appropriate to base the regional analysis on water regions because direct payments for water are relatively few and have only recently been included in the ASE.

Table 2.9 shows that most payments for electricity occur in the Northern Electric and Yorkshire Electric areas, and in Scotland. Payments for gas are also most common in these areas plus London, the MANWEB region (based in Manchester) and the NORWEB region (based in Newcastle). Yorkshire Electric region has more than twice the number of direct payments for water than any other area except South Wales. Deductions for overpayments are rather evenly distributed over the electricity board areas apart from Scotland. Scotland stands out as the region most likely to have had deductions for overpayment and Social Fund recovery and direct payments for Community Charge arrears. Deductions for the Social Fund are least likely in the Southern and SEEBOARD areas. Other geographical differences are that rent payments are most likely in London, MANWEB and Yorkshire, and direct payments for the Community Charge are most common in Northern, MANWEB and South Wales.

Direct payments for electricity vary from an average of £6.82 in the Midlands Electricity area to £13.27 in South Western Electricity area, as seen in Table 2.10. The South West region has a higher proportion of households who do not have access to gas and hence use electricity for heating as well as for appliances. This region and Scotland, which has similar large rural areas, have the lowest average payments for gas at £7.87 and £7.50 respectively. The range of gas payments is not so great, rising to £10.71.

Other types of payments and deduction, particularly mortgage payments, are higher in the London area than elsewhere. Mortgage payments are also high in the Southern and Seeboard areas reflecting the higher price of housing in these regions. In addition, rental payments are higher in London and Southern regions and the London area has the highest average payments for Community Charge arrears.

Combinations of direct deductions

Often people are in arrears for more than one item: this section describes those direct payments which occur together. Table 2.11 shows that most deductions occur singly (67 per cent), but 21 per cent occur two at a time and 13 per cent three or more at a time. The total number with deductions in May 1992 was 1,005,800 – 20 per cent of those on Income Support.

Table 2.9 Use of deductions from benefit by electricity board areas

	Electricity	Gas	Rent and amenity	Water	Community Charge	Mortgage interest	Overpayment	Social Fund	All others
	%	%	%	%	%	%	%	%	%
Northern Electric	19.9	12.7	10.0	4.3	15.1	2.9	7.4	8.6	2.9
Yorkshire Electric	14.6	11.0	10.4	18.7	4.2	10.0	9.7	9.0	15.7
Eastern Electric	3.5	5.5	5.1	10.3	4.5	12.9	6.5	5.6	7.1
London Electric	6.8	9.0	17.2	7.5	1.2	1.4	6.0	8.1	18.6
Southern Electric	3.3	3.0	2.1	2.8	0.9	5.7	3.7	3.0	7.1
East Midlands Electricity	1.1	6.6	7.0	6.7	2.1	7.1	8.6	7.0	0
South Western Electricity	3.2	2.2	2.9	4.6	1.8	5.7	4.9	3.7	8.6
Midlands Electricity	1.5	4.2	7.0	2.8	2.4	5.7	11.4	9.3	1.4
South Wales Electricity	1.6	7.6	1.2	15.9	8.0	8.6	5.2	5.1	12.9
MANWEB	6.7	10.5	11.2	11.2	13.9	20.0	6.3	9.7	1.4
NORWEB	1.8	10.0	8.0	11.2	5.3	5.7	10.8	9.0	4.3
SEEBOARD	3.3	3.2	1.4	3.1	1.8	10.0	3.8	3.1	8.6
Scotland	32.6	14.3	16.4	0.6	38.9	4.3	15.8	18.9	11.4

Source: Analysis of Income Support Statistics Annual Enquiry, May 1991

Table 2.10 Level of deductions by type of deduction and electricity board areas

Deduction	All cases	Northern Electric	Yorkshire Electric	Eastern Electric	London Electric	Southern electric	East Midlands Electric	South Western Electric	Midlands Electric	South Wales Electric	MANWEB	NORWEB	SEEBOARD	Scotland
	£ per week	£ per week	£ per week	£ per week	£ per week	£ per week	£ per week	£ per week	£ per week	£ per week	£ per week	£ per week	£ per week	£ per week
Electricity	9.86	8.23	9.97	9.78	9.92	10.69	10.23	13.27	6.82	8.76	9.69	10.72	10.32	10.50
Gas	9.31	9.77	8.78	9.94	9.25	9.49	10.71	7.87	10.06	9.63	9.20	10.60	9.03	7.50
Rent and amenity	3.81	2.12	3.29	4.05	5.63	6.59	4.82	2.73	2.79	3.49	3.36	3.76	3.33	2.20
Water	4.55	3.90	4.41	5.01	4.30	3.72	4.47	4.25	1.18	5.41	4.48	4.28	3.88	4.32
Community Charge	2.08	2.00	1.99	2.41	3.80	2.00	2.00	2.24	2.00	2.10	2.07	2.00	2.19	2.03
Mortgage interest	40.04	27.86	39.76	42.59	61.38	57.78	23.37	28.87	38.54	46.52	31.87	30.47	61.23	43.60
Overpayment	3.68	3.10	3.10	4.24	5.10	4.16	3.32	3.81	3.00	3.67	3.28	4.17	4.49	3.29
Social Fund	5.53	4.86	5.52	6.13	6.53	6.00	5.63	5.59	5.61	5.09	5.29	5.54	6.54	5.21
All others	29.91	24.16	7.57	99.79	24.67	41.69	0	3.13	5.24	14.72	3.57	99.99	58.44	15.39

Source: Analysis of Income Support Statistics Annual Enquiry, May 1991

Table 2.11 Recipients with different numbers of deductions, May 1992

Number of deductions	Number of recipients	Percentage of all recipients	Percentage of those with deductions
1	673,300	13	67
2	214,800	4	21
3	89,400	2	9
4	26,500	1	3
5	1,800	<1	<1
Total number of recipients with direct deductions	**1,005,800**		

Source: Analysis of Income Support Annual Enquiry, 1992

As Table 2.12 (section (a)) shows, by far the largest group of people among those with deductions (35 per cent) have one deduction for a Social Fund loan. The next largest group (11 per cent) consists of those with one deduction for Community Charge arrears. Any other combination accounts for less than five per cent of those with deductions from benefit. For example five per cent of those with deductions have one deduction for overpayment. Section (b) of the table sets out the most common combinations of deductions occurring two at a time. The percentages have not been presented because they are all small. For example, only four per cent of those with deductions have the most common pair of deductions for the Community Charge and Social Fund recovery. The other common combinations of two deductions also include Social Fund recovery, with gas for three per cent and with water for two per cent of those with deductions.

For combinations of three or more deductions (Table 2.12, section (c)) the combinations have only been presented if they occur in more than 1,000 cases. Among those with three deductions, the combination of direct payments for gas and electricity and a deduction for Social Fund recovery is the most common. Other combinations used by approximately 3,000 people are: electricity, gas and water; electricity, gas and Community Charge; and electricity, Community Charge and Social Fund recovery. Because of the priority ordering of direct payments the only combinations of four deductions which can occur must include Social Fund recovery, payment of the Community Charge or overpayment as one item. As Table 2.12 (section (d)) shows, the two most common combinations are: Social Fund recovery, payments for Community Charge, water and gas; Social Fund recovery, Community Charge, gas and electricity payments. A few people have five deductions and the most common combinations are listed in the last section (e) of the table.

Table 2.12 Combinations of deductions, May 1992

a. Only one deduction

Type of deduction	Numbers of cases	Percentage of those with deductions
Social Fund recovery	353,000	35
Community Charge	114,400	11
Overpayment recovery	47,100	5
Gas only	42,800	4
Water charges	34,000	3
Mortgage interest	30,400	3
Rent arrears/amenity	23,900	2
Electricity only	19,600	2
Other housing costs	5,500	1
Other: inc. residential and nursing homes, hostels, unpaid fines	2,600	<1
Total with only one deduction	**673,300**	**67**
Total with at least one deduction	**1,005,800**	

b. Combinations of two deductions only

Combination of deductions	Numbers of cases
Community Charge and Social Fund recovery	42,900
Gas and Social Fund recovery	31,400
Water and Social Fund recovery	18,900
Rent and Social Fund	15,900
Social Fund recovery and overpayment recovery	13,900
Electricity and Social Fund recovery	12,700
Rent and one other payment	11,000
Electricity and gas	10,100
Gas and water charges	9,500
Gas and one other payment	8,800
Gas and Community Charge	8,600
Electricity and one other payment	7,500
Water and Community Charge	6,800
Mortgage interest and one other payment	5,500
Water and one other payment	3,500
All other combinations of two payments	7,800
Total with only two deductions	**214,800** **(21 per cent)**

c. Combinations of three deductions

Combination of deductions	Numbers of cases
Electricity, gas, and Social Fund recovery	12,500
Gas, water and Social Fund recovery	9,500
Gas, Community Charge and Social Fund recovery	9,000
Water, Community Charge and Social Fund recovery	6,400
Gas, rent and Social Fund recovery	4,800
Rent, Community Charge and Social Fund recovery	4,200
Rent, water and Social Fund recovery	3,300
Gas, water and Community Charge	3,100
Electricity, Community Charge and Social Fund recovery	3,000
Electricity, gas and Community Charge	3,000
Electricity, gas and water charges	2,800
Electricity, rent or amenity arrears and Social Fund recovery	2,200
Community Charge, Social Fund and overpayment recovery	2,100
Electricity, gas and rent	1,900
Gas, Social Fund and overpayment recovery	1,800
Electricity, gas and one other payment	1,400
Electricity, water charges and Social Fund recovery	1,300
Electricity, Social Fund and overpayment recovery	1,100
Gas, rent and Community Charge	1,100
Gas, rent or amenity arrears and water charges	1,100
Rent, water, and Community Charge	1,100
Water, Community Charge and overpayment recovery	1,100
Gas, Community Charge and overpayment recovery	1,000
Water, Social Fund and overpayment recovery	1,000
All other combinations of three deductions	10,500
Total with only three deductions	**89,400** **(9 per cent)**

d. Combinations of four deductions

Combination of deductions	Numbers of cases
Social Fund recovery, Community Charge, water, gas	4,900
Social Fund recovery, Community Charge, gas, electricity	4,700
Social Fund recovery, water, rent/amenity, gas	2,500
Community Charge, water, gas, electricity	2,300
Social Fund recovery, Community Charge, rent/amenity, gas	1,200
Overpayment, Social Fund recovery, gas, electricity	1,100
Social Fund recovery, water, gas, electricity	1,000
All other combinations of four deductions	8,800
Total with four deductions	**26,500** **(3 per cent)**

e. Combinations of five deductions

Social Fund recovery, Community Charge, water, gas electricity	700
Social Fund, overpayment, Community Charge and two other payments	700
Other combinations	400
Total with five deductions	**1,800**
	(less than 1 per cent)

Source: Analysis of Income Support Annual Enquiry, 1992

Length of time on benefit

Two hypotheses might be proposed to explain the relationship between the length of time on benefit and the use of direct payments. For those starting on benefit, having had some other source of income, probably at a higher level, the longer they are on benefit the more difficult it is likely to be to meet essential commitments and replace goods as they wear out. For this reason it might be expected that the number of deductions would rise with length of time on benefit. A further reason might be that people learn that direct payments and deductions are available. In the case of the Social Fund, recipients can only apply after they have been on Income Support for six months. Not all are given a loan but knowledge of the scheme is a prerequisite of application. This is not necessarily true for direct payments since the initial application may come from a third-party creditor. Knowledge is less likely to be the main factor than the likely rise in debt with increased time on benefit. Table 2.13 shows that the numbers of deductions from benefit does increase with the length of time on benefit. The proportion with one deduction falls from 88 per cent for those who have been on Income Support for less than three months to 64 per cent for those who have been on for three years and more. Conversely, the proportions with three or more deductions rise from 2 per cent to 14 per cent as the length of time on benefit increases.

Table 2.13 Number of cases with deductions by length of time on Income Support

Number of deductions	Less than 3 months	3 to 6 months	6 to 12 months	1 to 2 years	2 to 3 years	3 years and over
	%	%	%	%	%	%
1	88	85	80	74	70	64
2	10	10	14	19	21	23
3	2	5	6	5	8	10
4 or more	0	<1	1	2	1	3
All deductions	**5**	**7**	**15**	**18**	**10**	**45**
N	**32,900**	**48,300**	**104,400**	**120,100**	**70,200**	**305,600**

Source: Analysis of Income Support Annual Enquiry, 1991

Earlier tables have shown the level of deduction for each kind of direct payment or deduction. However the previous section (Table 2.11) shows that a third of those with deductions from benefit have more than one. Table 2.14 shows the average level of deductions for given combinations of deductions. We are mainly presenting combinations of two deductions, and only the more common of three or more deductions. The combination of a payment for electricity and a deduction for the Social Fund results in the highest level of deduction, £16.14 per week among the combinations of two deductions irrespective of the time on benefit. The average levels for three or four deductions are higher. The cumulative deduction for those with deductions for electricity, gas, rent and the Social Fund amounts to £24.37 per week. Relatively few have this combination of deductions, but a considerable number have deductions for electricity, gas and the Social Fund amounting to £21.06 per week.

Table 2.14 Level of deductions for most common combinations of deductions by length of time on Income Support

Combinations of deductions	Less than 3 months	3 to 6 months	6 to 12 months	1 to 2 years	2 to 3 years	3 years and over	All cases	N
	£ per week	£ per week	£ per week	£ per week	£ per week	£ per week	£ per week	
Gas and electricity	17.92	14.10	15.89	16.47	19.10	14.61	15.41	**12,600**
Gas and water	18.19	17.76	14.85	14.72	12.83	14.49	14.62	**6,700**
Gas and rent	12.29	16.00	12.92	12.08	13.54	12.53	12.59	**5,300**
Gas and Social Fund	12.80	17.63	14.80	13.99	14.29	14.76	14.69	**25,900**
Rent and Social Fund	8.99	7.40	9.47	9.06	8.59	9.31	9.11	**17,800**
Electricity and Social Fund	24.96	14.70	16.54	16.98	17.12	15.55	16.14	**14,700**
Water and Social Fund	11.50	9.92	8.93	10.68	11.14	10.12	10.24	**12,300**
Overpayment and Social Fund	12.98	7.61	7.91	8.11	9.03	7.88	8.24	**9,600**
Community Charge and Social Fund	6.32	4.88	7.77	6.85	7.25	7.42	7.22	**6,800**
Electricity, gas and rent	20.50	17.26	22.16	14.20	21.54	18.54	19.08	**3,100**
Electricity, gas and Social Fund	0	19.13	23.17	22.03	20.84	20.53	21.06	**11,200**
Electricity, gas, rent and Social Fund	0	0	29.25	25.68	14.64	24.24	24.37	**4,100**

Source: Analysis of Annual Statistical Enquiry, 1991

Use of direct payments and other deductions by respondents in the national sample of Income Support recipients

This section outlines the total number of deductions from benefit experienced by the sample in the national survey of Income Support recipients. In this survey recipients were asked what deductions from benefit they had in the six month interval from the 1st of August 1992 to the time of the interviews in February or March 1993. Table 2.15 compares the use of direct payments by the sample with the national figures for May 1992. The proportions with any given deduction are generally higher in the sample than in the ASE partly because the ASE figures are almost a year older than those from the sample. Also, the sample figures may include some deductions which are no longer current, as it covers a six-month interval. The most obvious difference is in deductions for rent. It is not clear why this should be, as it seems unlikely that debts for rent should be cleared more quickly than other debts. One possible explanation is that a few people in the survey have interpreted Housing Benefit as a direct payment for rent. The proportions with direct payments for Community Charge arrears is also much higher in the sample than in the ASE but this is more readily explicable by the later timing of the survey and the consequent greater likelihood of Community Charge arrears. Apart from these differences the proportions with different types of direct deductions are broadly similar in the ASE and the sample survey.

Table 2.15 Analysis of direct payments: comparison of Annual Statistical Enquiry, May 1992, with survey results

Deduction	Number of cases		Percent of recipients	
	ASE	Sample	ASE	Sample
Electricity	95,000	30	2	3
Gas	192,000	53	4	5
Rent arrears/amenity	85,000	98	2	9
Water charges	132,000	50	3	4
Community Charge	243,000	107	5	9
Mortgage interest	44,000	57	1	5
Other housing costs	14,000	–	0	–
Residential care/nursing home fees	1,000	–	0	–
Hostel charges	1,000	–	0	–
Unpaid fines recovery	–	1	0	–
Social Fund recovery	586,000	103	12	9
Overpayments recovery	92,000	10	2	1
All recipients	**5,088,000**	**1,137**		

Source: Survey of Income Support recipients and ASE, May 1992

Comparison of the sample and national figures on the numbers of deductions in Table 2.16 shows that the distribution of people with different numbers of deductions among those with deductions is similar for the sample and the ASE. The estimated proportion of those on Income Support with deductions is, as expected, higher among the sample survey of recipients than in the ASE, particularly for those with one deduction.

Table 2.16 Recipients with different numbers of deductions: comparison of Annual Statistical Enquiry, May 1992, with survey results

Number of deductions	Number of recipients		Percentage of all recipients		Percentage of those with deductions	
	ASE	Sample	ASE	Sample	ASE	Sample
1	673,300	198	13	17	67	63
2	214,800	63	4	6	21	20
3	89,400	36	2	3	9	11
4	26,500	12	1	1	3	4
5	1,800	7	<1	1*	1	2
Total number of recipients with direct deductions	**1,005,800**	**316**				

* Percentage based on fewer than ten cases

Source: Survey of Income Support recipients and ASE, May 1992

Conclusion

This chapter has set the context for the study using information from administrative statistics to show the extensive use of direct payments and deductions. A fifth of Income Support recipients have at least one direct payment or deduction. Lone parents are particularly likely to have direct payments or deductions, and their use of the schemes seems to be of a different order to others. The likelihood of having increasing numbers of deductions and of having larger amounts deducted from benefit rises with length of time on benefit.

The use of direct payments and deductions by the sample of Income Support recipients in the survey compares fairly closely with that given by administrative data. In general, the proportions with different types of deductions are similar in the ASE and the survey, apart from higher proportions in the survey with deductions for rent and Community Charge arrears. The proportions with different numbers of deductions are also similar in

LIVERPOOL JOHN MOORES UNIVERSITY
Aldham Roberts L.R.C.
TEL. 051 231 3701/3634

the ASE and the sample survey. Thus results from the survey presented in subsequent chapters can be considered to be broadly representative of users of direct payments and deductions.

Chapter 3 Coming on to Direct Payment Schemes

Introduction

As part of our research brief we were asked to explore the behaviour and experience of Income Support recipients prior to applying for direct payments and examine the reasons why some are refused. Specifically, we were requested to address the following issues:

- identify the needs that contribute to the move to direct payments and explore how these needs arose

- review people's coping strategies prior to using direct payments

- examine whether any problems are experienced in getting accepted on to direct payment schemes

- explore people's attitudes to direct payments that are imposed

- identify the number and types of Income Support recipients who are refused direct payments, and

- examine the reasons why direct payments are refused.

This chapter discusses each of these and outlines the policy implications arising from the findings.

Factors contributing to the move to direct payments

Direct payments are intended to assist Income Support recipients in financial difficulties to meet their financial obligations to third parties by diverting an amount of their benefit at source to pay for arrears and current consumption. To appreciate the reasons why some recipients use direct payments, it is important to understand the contributory factors that cause recipients to experience financial difficulties and default on payments to third parties. The analysis presented in this chapter is based on interviews with 45 Income Support recipients and provides explanations and illustrations of the processes involved within the sample group.

Our research identified five principal causes of default by recipients: low income; changes in circumstances; lack of money management skills; withholding of payment; and the practices of third parties. For some Income Support recipients default was the result of a combination of these factors.

Low income

Households living on a low, fixed income and eking out a tight budget have a limited capacity to absorb a large draw upon their finances. The qualitative interviews revealed that for many people (approximately half of the sample) the primary cause of arrears was a large household bill that could not be met from current income or savings. Some causes of default (over half of the sample) were not necessarily unexpected and arose from the difficulties of routinely matching a limited budget to longer term commitments. We found that some respondents were continuously having to 'rob Peter to pay Paul' in order to meet basic household commitments, and some walked a precarious financial tightrope between solvency and debt. From our interviews it emerged that short-term contingencies, such as the need to replace damaged shoes, sometimes took precedence over regular commitments such as payment of rent.

For some households, even the smallest deviation from essential household budgeting commitments could result in arrears. A single parent with two children explained that if she spent some of the money originally devoted to household bills on an outing for her children, she would find it almost impossible to repay this money at a later date:

> *Because with people who are on Income Support and low incomes, there's, how can I say, some weeks hard like to live and you just spend the money, I know it doesn't seem much but you spend it if the kids are in all day like this, you'll say 'oh sod it I'll take them to the pictures today'. Where people who are working like automatically, even if it's not a high income, can afford these things. Like today, if it's raining and your kids have got nothing doing, then sod it you think you'll make it back up, or well I'll put it back in next week, but it doesn't, it just gets bigger and bigger and you can't always put it back in. (Ms A)*

Many people on similar levels of income manage to budget and do not default on financial commitments. Berthoud and Kempson (1992) show that low income alone is not a simple explanation for debt. In their survey (standardising for income) younger age groups and families with children were most likely to default on payments.

Changes in circumstances

The qualitative interviews revealed that unemployment, or a relationship breakdown, were contributory factors to defaulting on household bills for some respondents. Most respondents had taken on credit commitments such as catalogue purchases when they had been in a position to meet repayments, and a sudden reduction in income made servicing these credit agreements difficult. For other households, normal fluctuations in income and expenditure culminated in arrears. Several respondents had tried to repay loans for consumer goods by cutting back on basic household expenses such as fuel and housing costs. Others reported that they paid door-to-door money lenders before paying for household commitments. A number of respondents reported that their financial difficulties began after their partners had left, leaving them to pay all the household bills. For some respondents an unexpected increase in expenditure to cover an urgent, acute problem such as replacing a lost coat precipitated financial difficulties.

Lack of money management and budgeting skills

Some respondents reported that their financial problems were due to their own general lack of money management and budgeting skills although Berthoud and Kempson (1992) found no evidence to suggest that low-income households were any more likely to lack budgeting skills than those on higher incomes. Whereas individuals on higher incomes may equally lack financial skills, those managing on a low income have a greater likelihood of experiencing financial difficulties.

A few respondents were very candid about their perceived lack of budgeting skills and blamed themselves for defaulting on payment. An unemployed man with arrears for rent, gas and the Community Charge explained that his financial situation was a result of the inability to manage his money:

> *I'm terrible with my money, I'm one of these people who thinks, Oh well I've got to pay this week, but I won't bother paying that until next week sort of thing and then I won't pay it until the week after ... I am absolutely useless when it comes down to paying bills ... I always have been, I've got absolutely no financial control at all. (Mr A)*

Some respondents reported that they had visited a Citizens Advice Bureau and received advice about household budgeting.

Withholding of payment

Traditionally, debtors have either been classified as those who *cannot* pay and those who *will not* pay their financial commitments. Those who withhold payments were sometimes viewed as dishonest or fraudulent by creditors. The in-depth interviews revealed that some Income Support recipients accrue arrears because they purposefully withhold payments to third parties. Two respondents in the qualitative survey reported that they did not pay their Community Charge because they were opposed to the tax on political grounds and one respondent reported that he had accrued rent arrears because of a 'rent strike' organised in response to an increase in council property rents. In these examples, withholding of payment is more closely associated with personal and political interests, rather than a desire to defraud the local council. Direct payments in this situation effectively serve a judicial rather than a social function, by serving the interests of third parties against the personal wishes of recipients.

Practices of third-party creditors

The practices of third-party creditors may contribute to recipients defaulting on payments. Within the literature on debt, third-party practices such as irresponsible lending, excessive interest charges, and inappropriate payment methods, are identified as potential causes of increases in arrears. The qualitative interviews with respondents revealed that inappropriate payment and collection methods are a contributory factor to default. In one area the council policy of using door-to-door collection of rent money has resulted in some people unintentionally defaulting on their rent, for example, they are out when the rent collector calls.

A single, unemployed man explained that he accrued arrears because he was absent from his home on employment training when the rent collector visited.

> *I was never in on a Monday morning, nine o'clock when the rent man got here. So I couldn't pay him because he just wasn't here, I just wasn't here and he only came on a Monday, he wouldn't come any other time, like four o'clock or something like that. (Mr B)*

Similarly, a disabled, married man explains that rent payments did not accord with his cycle of budgeting. When the rent was due he had spent the money on other things.

> *By the time you get paid on a Monday, by the time Friday comes, and he comes to collect his money, you've spent it. (Mr C)*

Although this recipient may be accused of poor budgeting, his rent arrears might have been prevented if the rent collector had called when he had the money available. Chapter Five shows that many local authorities are increasingly adapting their payment practices to reduce the possibility of arrears.

In addition we also found that the practice of fuel companies to estimate fuel consumption culminated in arrears for some people. One woman had accrued a bill for £800 because the fuel company had underestimated her consumption over the period of a year. While it is the responsibility of the customer to notify fuel companies of under-estimation, in practice some people will not do so because it provides additional financial flexibility in the short term, although at the expense of long-term budgeting.

For the majority of Income Support recipients in our small sample, low income was an underlying factor if not always the principal reason for default. Many had defaulted on payments because of the pressures and demands of eking out a tight budget. The route into debt for these people was often gradual and took many months. However, people's financial problems were most acute when low income combined with a change in household circumstances such as the breakdown of a relationship. In these situations the route into debt was often more sudden and associated with a crisis. By contrast, fewer respondents had defaulted because of the practices of creditors, or because they lacked money management skills. Although several had withheld payments to third parties, this was more closely associated with political action than an attempt at fraud.

People's coping strategies prior to direct payments

Before starting direct payments the financial situations of our respondents varied widely. Some had substantial arrears to a number of third parties which had gradually

LIVERPOOL JOHN MOORES UNIVERSITY
LEARNING SERVICES

increased over many months, whereas others had commenced direct payments soon after incurring sufficient arrears to qualify.

Respondents also varied in the strategies adopted to cope with their financial situation. These ranged from doing nothing, to making a payment arrangement with the third party, to clearing the outstanding arrears.

Several respondents had tried a weekly or fortnightly budget account with the creditor, but had failed to keep to the agreed payments and had been taken off the scheme. Others had tried to get an alternative payment method, such as a gas pre-payment meter, but had been refused. In these situations they sometimes reported that the creditor contacted the Benefits Agency on their behalf to request a direct payment. Several reported that the threat of an eviction or disconnection spurred them to seek direct payments. The majority of people in the qualitative survey (42 respondents) reported that they had not attempted to borrow to pay off the arrears, although two had been refused a Social Fund loan. Some had sought help from a local Citizens Advice Bureau, or welfare rights agency, and were informed by them about the availability of direct payment schemes. Several respondents reported that they adopted a strategy of delaying payments until the very last moment prior to sanctions taking place.

The process of being accepted on to direct payments

The Benefits Agency is committed to providing a high quality service for all potential and actual Income Support recipients. We were therefore concerned to explore their experiences of applying for direct payments and to identify specific problems that they had.

The qualitative survey showed variations in the experiences of being accepted onto direct payment schemes. Some people were generally pleased with the way that the Benefits Agency had dealt with them and could not think of ways in which the process could be improved. Others reported problems which either related to the length of time they had to wait before notification that direct payments were to be implemented, or to mistakes by the Benefits Agency when paying third-party creditors.

Generally, we found that for many respondents the transition to direct payments was a smooth and trouble-free experience. Indeed some recipients were very complimentary about the standard of service provided, often at a time of crisis for them, by the Benefits Agency.

A pensioner described in glowing terms her experience of coming on to direct payments:

> *They were really fantastic I'm telling you ... they were marvellous believe you me, they were as helpful as they could ever be to me... If anyone tells me the social are not all right there is something wrong with them. (Ms B)*

For other recipients the transition to direct payments was rather more problematic. A lone parent who had found out about direct payments from a Citizens Advice Bureau, explained that the length of time she had to wait between applying for direct payments and the adjudication officer's decision (3 months), left her anxious, and worried that her water supply would be disconnected.

> *I contacted the DSS. It took quite a long time to come through. They were going to cut the water off and all the rest of it, so at that time I was a bit worried. I think it is a good idea but I think it takes too long to come through and it leaves you on the edge ... You know, thinking am I going to get it, am I going to get cut off? (Ms C)*

A single, unemployed man explained that he encountered problems because, although the Benefits Agency was making deductions for arrears of rent, the money was not being credited to his rent account.

> *I had a couple of problems to start off with, the fact that I was getting letters saying that I was still in arrears and it has sort of sorted itself out now. But it*

started off where it was a pain, sort of like getting these letters saying 'Your rent hasn't been paid'. (Mr C)

The Benefits Agency, as part of the Joint Statement of Intent with the fuel and water companies, does have maximum response times for dealing with direct payment applications. However our survey shows that these have not prevented some people from experiencing anxiety and stress while waiting for decisions.

Knowledge of direct payments

Current policy regarding direct payments is to target 'information at the point of need'. To assess the effectiveness of this policy it is necessary to assess the proportion of those in 'need' who actually know about direct payments. In our questionnaire survey we asked about how people were managing their finances. Table 3.1 shows the responses to this question for recipients who were not currently using direct payments. This table shows that over two-thirds of recipients, who were not currently using direct payments, and who reported they were getting into or already had budgeting difficulties, did not know about direct payments. Although some of these people would not wish to use direct payments or would not be eligible, it appears that some people who are experiencing budgeting difficulties do not know of direct payments as a potential method of assistance.

Table 3.1   Perceived budgeting difficulties by knowledge of direct payment schemes (Income Support recipients not currently using direct payments)

Perception of how managing money	Total	Number lacking knowledge of direct payments	%
No problems	121	104	(86)
Just getting by/coping	505	379	(75)
Getting into difficulties	104	75	(72)
Already in difficulties	73	49	(67)
N	**803**		

Source: Questionnaire Survey

However, our findings also show that the majority of Income Support recipients (63 per cent) who perceive themselves to be in budgeting difficulties either know about direct payments or are currently using them.

Knowledge about the existence of direct payments also differs markedly between claimant types. Of those survey respondents who were not currently using direct payments, pensioners and disabled people were much less likely to know about them than the unemployed and lone parents (Table 3.2). Whereas almost nine out of ten pensioners and more than four out of five disabled recipients lacked knowledge about direct payments, just over half of lone parents were in this situation. As we have shown in the previous chapter, lone parents are most likely and pensioners least likely to use direct payments.

Table 3.2   Knowledge of direct payments among those not currently using them (by claimant type)

	Unemployed	Lone parent	Pensioners	Sick/ disabled	Other	All
	%	%	%	%	%	%
Knew	31	48	12	19	40	25
Did not know	69	52	88	81	60	75
N	**280**	**117**	**293**	**101**	**30**	**821**

Source: Questionnaire Survey

In the survey we tried to get an indication of the potential use of direct payment schemes among people who had not heard of them. As Table 3.3 shows, over a quarter of unemployed people and lone parents said they might have applied to get on one of the schemes had they known, in contrast to only one in ten pensioners and sick and disabled people. These figures most likely reflect the relatively stable financial circumstances of pensioners and disabled people compared with the unemployed and lone parents. That so many pensioners (79 per cent) said they would *not* have tried to get on a scheme probably also reflects the dislike of indebtedness common among older people.

Table 3.3 Potential use of direct payments among people who had no knowledge of schemes

Might have used if known	All	Unemployed	Lone parents	Pensioners	Sick/ disabled
	%	%	%	%	%
Yes	17	26	30	10	12
No	71	66	62	79	67
Do not know	11	8	8*	12	21
N	614	194	61	259	82

* Based on fewer than 10 cases
Source: Questionnaire Survey

The qualitative interviews also revealed that people on direct payments sometimes lacked knowledge about the full range of schemes. In particular many did not know about payments for Community Charge arrears.

Our interviews with Benefits Agency staff suggest that some are also unaware of the availability of information about direct payments. Although an information leaflet (IS9) which explains how direct payments operate has been available since June 1992, none of the staff interviewed in the three local offices visited during the spring and summer of 1993 had heard of it.

The supervisor of the direct payments section in area 2 stated that:

> *To be honest with you as regards to the direct payment scheme, as far as I'm aware there aren't any leaflets that specifically explain it.*

If staff do not know of the availability of information leaflets they cannot effectively publicise direct payment schemes. The Benefits Agency should therefore consider investigating further the level of knowledge that staff have of them.

Sources of information about direct payments

Of the people in the survey who knew about direct payments and deductions, most had first heard about them from the DSS (Table 3.4). This is not surprising given that new Income Support claimants are informed about direct payment for mortgage interest soon after their claim is received, and the Benefits Agency also contact recipients about direct payments for Community Charge arrears and rent arrears.

Table 3.4 Sources of information about direct payments

	N	Percentage
DSS	296	57
Friend/relative	143	27
Creditor	36	7
Other	26	5
Media	15	3
Money adviser	15	3
Don't know	2	–
N	523	100

Source: Questionnaire Survey

The table also shows that informal networks of family and friends are an important source of information for a sizeable minority of people (27 per cent), a finding confirmed in the qualitative interviews.

Attitudes towards the levying of direct payments

Although Income Support recipients may request the Benefits Agency to arrange direct payments, they can also be implemented without such a request. Whether direct payments are levied or chosen is likely to affect the acceptability of schemes. One might expect a higher level of satisfaction about coming onto a scheme among recipients who had asked for a direct payment than those who had one levied.

Our questionnaire survey revealed that the majority of direct payments (63 per cent) are levied rather than requested by recipients. Whether direct payments are levied also seems to vary between claimant groups. We found that unemployed claimants were more likely to have direct payments levied than other categories of claimants. For unemployed claimants over 70 per cent of direct payments were levied compared with 50–60 per cent for other categories of claimant.

Apart from direct payments for mortgage interest which are automatically implemented, payments for Community Charge arrears were most likely to be levied, and payments for gas and electricity the least (Table 3.5). What is surprising from these figures is the high proportion of people who believed they had requested to have direct payments for mortgage interest, Community Charge arrears and rent arrears. Some of the sample may have opted to use direct payments for mortgage interest prior to it becoming compulsory in 1992. Currently however, only local authorities are successful in requests for rent and Community Charge arrears. One interpretation of these figures is that people were generally in agreement with the decision by the council to seek direct payments.

Table 3.5 Perceptions of whether direct payments were requested or levied, by type of scheme

	Gas	Electricity	Water	Rent	Mortgage	Community Charge	Other
	%	%	%	%	%	%	%
Requested	55	35	48	35	23	31	25*
Levied	45	62	48	62	77	69	58
Don't know	–	3*	4*	3*	–	–	17*
N	**53**	**29**	**50**	**98**	**56**	**105**	**24**

* Based on fewer than 10 cases
Source: Questionnaire Survey

The qualitative interviews revealed that recipients are not necessarily dissatisfied when direct payments are levied. Indeed, almost all the recipients in the qualitative survey who had direct payments levied by the Benefits Agency wished to continue using direct payments, even those who disagreed with the original imposition. No one in the qualitative survey had appealed against the imposition of a direct payment.

Refusal of direct payments

An important element in monitoring the accessibility of direct payment schemes is to identify when and why people are not accepted on to a scheme by an adjudication officer. In the year to September 1993, almost a quarter (23 per cent) of requests by Income Support recipients and third-party creditors were refused (Table 3.6).

Refusal rates differ according to the type of direct payment sought. Over twice as many requests for fuel direct payments were refused compared with requests for child support, rent and fines.

Table 3.6   Requests and refusals for direct payment, October 1992 to September 1993

Type of direct payment	Number of requests	% Refused
Community Charge	419,206	23
Fuel	127,403	31
Water	93,421	16
Rent	54,478	15
Others	10,974	23
Child support	4,784	15
Fines	4,080	14
Council Tax	1032	27
Total	**715,387**	**23**

Source: Benefits Agency Local Office Statistics

In our questionnaire survey five per cent of respondents had been refused direct payments over the previous six months. This disparity may be explained largely by the fact that our sample only included recipients who were on Income Support. One of the main reasons for refusal is that the person for whom direct payments is requested is not on Income Support. In addition, we also found evidence to indicate that refusals to third-party creditors are often higher than refusals to individuals. Benefits Agency staff in area 2 for example estimated that on average five per cent of requests from recipients and 15 per cent of requests from third parties are refused. Similarly, in area 3, staff estimated that on average five to ten per cent of requests from recipients were refused compared with up to 50 per cent of requests from creditors. The high refusal rate for creditors was largely explained by utilities, particularly water companies, requesting direct payments for people not currently on Income Support.

Reasons for refusal

Interviews with local Benefits Agency staff indicated that there were four principal reasons for refusing direct payments: applications for people not currently on Income Support; the existence of a viable alternative payment method; insufficient income; and insufficient arrears.

Application for person not on Income Support

Benefits Agency staff reported that the most common reason for refusing direct payments was because applications came from, or for, people not currently on Income Support. It was reported that these requests usually came from third parties rather than individuals. Chapter Six shows that in order to reduce the number of ineligible applications, some local authorities now link the information that they have about Housing Benefit with information about tenants with rent arrears.

Alternative methods of payment available

Adjudication officers have the discretion to refuse requests for direct payments where an alternative method of payment is available. Staff reported that this reason for refusal most commonly applied to recipients seeking fuel direct. In particular, unemployed, single people and lone parents with older children were the most likely claimant groups to be refused direct payments because the adjudication officer believed that a viable alternative payment method, such as a pre-payment meter, existed. Most staff believed that pre-payment meters were not a viable option for pensioners, disabled people and families with young children and consequently few of these claimant groups were refused direct payments for this reason.

Insufficient income or arrears

Applicants for direct payments might be refused because they have insufficient available income after deductions have been made or because there are insufficient arrears. The adjudication officer in area 2 reported that refusals because arrears were too small particularly applied to requests from the city council for direct payment for rent arrears. In September 1993, almost a quarter of requests for rent direct were refused for this reason.

The direct payments supervisor in area 3 reported that refusals because of insufficient income were usually connected with requests for Community Charge arrears. In August 1993, almost a quarter of requests for Community Charge arrears to be paid by direct payments were refused in area 3 because recipients were deemed to have insufficient income. Staff in all three areas thought that a few recipients were refused direct payments because they were already paying the maximum possible number of direct payments.

Summary and policy implications

Most respondents in our qualitative sample found that coming on to direct payments was a straightforward procedure once a request had been made, and were generally pleased with the service provided by the Benefits Agency.

However, some people did experience problems, such as waiting for long periods for an adjudication officer's decision about acceptance on to a scheme. This could cause anxiety and stress for recipients, particularly if third parties were pressing in their demands for payment.

At present the Benefits Agency do not have target response times for direct payments and the introduction of these could lead to a higher standard of service. Better communication between the Benefits Agency and creditors could also help reduce problems.

When administering direct payments, the adjudication officer becomes the central figure in a three-way communication. Perhaps a greater recognition of this would lead to the adjudication officer 'taking ownership' of a case and ensuring, through good communication, that everything runs smoothly. Such a move would be in the general spirit of the 'one-stop' approach to service delivery, currently being developed by the Benefits Agency.

The current policy to provide direct payments only as a 'last resort' and target information 'at the point of need' is reflected in the qualifying conditions and the publicity strategy. Our research suggests that many people who could benefit from direct payments do not know about them and that many people not on Income Support apply to use them. This necessarily raises questions about the effectiveness of the Department's current information strategy. However, any policy to publicise more widely the availability of schemes to Income Support recipients should avoid raising expectations among this population.

Chapter 4   Experience of Using Direct Payments

This chapter considers whether those on direct payments find them useful and are satisfied with the way they are administered. Findings are presented from both the survey and qualitative interviews on what is most valued and most problematic about the use of direct payments from benefit as a method of payment for arrears.

This chapter addresses the following issues identified in the research proposal:

- the effect of direct payments on the ability to budget
- whether those using the schemes were content with the information they had received and the help given by DSS staff, and
- whether direct payments for current expenditure (for fuel and metered water) cause problems.

The first section presents the evidence for the advantages of the schemes, and the second discusses some of the problems. Before addressing detailed issues, however, it should be recorded that almost all of the respondents to the qualitative interviews were pleased with the direct payments they were using. Thus direct payments do seem to provide a generally useful and satisfactory service.

Advantages of direct payments

Many advantages of direct payments are noted in the literature and these were outlined in the introduction and are summarised in the following list. In this section we discuss each in turn.

The advantages of direct payments are:

- protection from creditor sanctions – in particular, safeguarding essential utility supplies (gas, electricity and water) and prevention of loss of home through eviction or repossession
- help with budgeting
- prioritising of payments
- payments spread evenly over the year
- help with mobility and access problems
- often cheaper than other methods.

Protection from sanctions

The list of sanctions for non-payment of debts for various supplies and services is long and the sanctions can be severe. Fuel and water supplies can be disconnected, and homes repossessed or tenants evicted if payments are not made on time. People can be left without the means to heat or light their homes. Codes of practice agreed with the regulators govern the disconnection of a fuel supply, the key conditions of which are: that repayment arrangements should take account of the customer's ability to pay when debt repayment arrangements are made; and that people should be offered a pre-payment meter before disconnection. A court order is not required before a company makes a disconnection. The codes cannot be enforced by an individual and only persistent breach of a code would result in the loss of a licence.

In the case of water supplies, water companies are required in almost every case to use the county court and obtain a court order to recover debt, but the water supply to a home can also be disconnected. Loss of water supply to the home has become a more common sanction since the privatisation of the water supply industry.

Debt for housing costs can lead to homelessness. Mortgage lenders can seek a repossession order on the property and landlords can evict tenants. Guidelines for dealing with debt have been prepared by the Council of Mortgage Lenders and these suggest a number of devices available to lenders to help borrowers in arrears difficulties. The help is limited, however, to relying on 'good practice' which might have little impact on less responsible lenders. Failure to pay the Community Charge or Council Tax can result in repossession of goods, and, in the final resort, imprisonment.

Many respondents in the qualitative interviews reported that direct payments had prevented creditors from enforcing sanctions. For example, Mr A, an unemployed man with direct payments for rent, gas, and water, explained that having built up large arrears to British Gas, he arranged a budget payment but failed to keep it. British Gas had threatened to disconnect if he would not accept direct payments.

> *I was in difficulty with the gas, it was the gas that was the worst one. And they was threatening to cut me off you know and they wouldn't let me get another budget scheme out again, I'd had it out once and I'd let them down. (Mr A)*

In some cases arranging direct payments had prevented disconnection but at the cost of worry and stress. Because of Benefits Agency delays there was sometimes a period of uncertainty about whether disconnection would happen or not.

> *I got into quite a lot of arrears with water bills...What happened is, the old flat I was in, the person I was living with left and left me with all the bills so I owed about a hundred and fifty pounds and then it just escalated from there. I contacted the DSS. It took quite a long time for it to come through – they were going to cut the water off...so at the time I was a bit worried...I think it was a good idea but I think it takes too long to come through and it leaves you on the edge. You know, thinking am I going to get it, am I going to get cut off? (Ms C, single parent)*

The qualitative interviews showed that those with direct payments were generally aware of the risk of disconnection for fuel and water and valued direct payments in preventing these outcomes. Although no-one interviewed talked of an immediate experience or threat of eviction or possession, respondents were aware of the possibility of losing their homes.

Help with budgeting

Direct payments can help with budgeting and prioritising payment for essential services although they only become an option after people are in debt. They operate as a rescue device rather than a preventive measure.

It is interesting to see how far direct payments can ameliorate problems of debt arising from a variety of situations. One cause of debt is a change in circumstances such as a partner leaving, as described in the example above. In such cases, going on to direct payments can clear a debt and provide the time to re-establish budgeting strategies in the new circumstances.

Another cause of debt is long-term, low income, and in these circumstances direct payments can ensure that essentials are paid for. For example:

> *Respondent:*   *I found the money I was getting for the mortgage in my Income Support I was spending, and not paying the mortgage because there was always something else to pay. And having got into arrears with the mortgage it was deemed by myself and the building society that we should go for a direct payment from the DSS.*

> *Interviewer:*   *What did you do with the money the DSS gave you for the mortgage?*

> *Respondent:* Well I'd use it, you know, to buy food or to pay for other bills, telephone, electricity, water board, they all come in you know. And obviously if we needed any, like my son needed shoes or anything like that, you bought those, you know, rather than pay the bills that were sitting in the background shall we say. Well we now know that certain parts of our budgeting is done for us, so we know what money's going to come in each fortnight and we can actually budget as to what we have to spend on food and what we can put away for things like shirts and shoes for the kids and also what we put away for other small bills. We still don't pay all the bills because there's just not enough money. And I mean we don't have a grand lifestyle, we live on a very meagre ration to be perfectly honest.
> *(Mr D, unemployed man with wife and two children)*

Mr D also pointed out that direct payments operated in the same way as direct debits from a bank account, the system he had been used to when he was in work. He felt that payment of bills by direct debit should be an option whether or not people were in work: in either case it meant that there was no worry about bills being paid on time.

A lone parent with two children and direct payments for gas, rent and water described how these helped her to budget despite pressure from her children. She said that if the children badgered her all day she might give in and take them to the pictures, saying to herself that she would make up the cost later but knowing it was unlikely.

Direct payments can ensure the continued supply of essentials even when people have difficulty managing their money adequately. For example, a single man with direct payments for rent, gas and the Community Charge said that direct payments had helped him because he felt he was 'absolutely useless' about paying bills.

A single parent with payments for gas and water provides a further example of the value of direct payments to someone who has difficulty managing her money:

> *...you see I'm a drinker as well...so if I have money I'd only spend it on drink. And that's being honest with you, you know, so I'd rather them have all me bills, I mean it was a good job I was off the drink to sort the gas out and the electric, otherwise everything would have gone to pot. (Ms D)*

A single man gives an example of how useful people found direct payments for budgeting:

> *What you don't have you don't miss. It's easy, you know exactly what's left, most of what you've got to pay out has already been paid out. So what you've got left you've got to budget on haven't you...I think it's a brilliant idea because anyone can be tempted to spend the money and you don't think about the consequences do you, specially when you're short of money anyway.*
> *(Mr E, single man)*

In all of these cases direct payments can be considered to be a help with budgeting. The help is limited, however, to ensuring the supply of essential services possibly at the cost of other only marginally less important goods. We saw above how Mr D had a choice between paying the mortgage and buying new shoes for his children. Direct payment ensures that the mortgage is paid and the house is not repossessed, but new shoes for children, in his view, presented an even more pressing need.

Respondents to the survey with a direct payment or deduction from benefit were asked how their household budgeting had been affected by the reduced amount of cash-in-hand. Table 4.1 shows the responses.

Table 4.1 Effect of direct payments on household budgeting

Effect	Type of direct payment								
	Gas	Elec	Water	Rent	Mortgage	Comm. charge	Deduc- tions[1]	Other	All
	%	%	%	%	%	%	%	%	%
Much worse	19	10*	15*	5*	9*	10	24	26*	14
A little worse	8*	17*	10*	5*	13*	29	36	35	20
No effect	13*	10*	16*	22	41	25	19	13*	21
A bit easier	36	48	33	40	18	26	15	13*	27
A lot easier	25	14*	25	27	20	10	6*	9*	16
N	53	30	50	98	57	107	113	23	532

* Fewer than 10 cases
1 Deductions for overpayment and Social Fund recovery

Overall, around 60 per cent of those with direct payments for gas, electricity, water and rent felt it had made budgeting easier. A quarter of those with a direct payment for gas or water or rent felt that it had made their budgeting a lot easier, as did a fifth of those with a direct payment for mortgage interest. Fewer felt that direct payments for electricity had helped to this extent. Only 38 per cent and 36 per cent of those with direct payments for mortgage interest and Community Charge respectively felt they had helped. Not surprisingly, 40 per cent of those with direct payments for mortgage interest felt they made no difference. The direct payment for mortgage interest is more like Housing Benefit and less of a deduction from benefit. Many of those with direct payments for mortgage interest might not be in arrears. Whether the Benefits Agency pays or they pay themselves, evidence from qualitative work suggests they feel they can manage to budget for their mortgage quite successfully (NACAB, 1993a). The proportions (between a fifth and a quarter) who feel that direct payments have made budgeting worse are similar for gas, electricity, water, and mortgage. Relatively few (fewer than ten cases for each of these payments) said direct payments had made budgeting much worse. However, nearly 40 per cent said the direct payment of Community Charge arrears has made it more difficult to budget. This could reflect attitudes to the payment of a tax rather than effects on budgeting as discussed in Chapter Three. Such an influence is more clearly at work in the attitudes to paying other deductions from benefit for repayments for a Social Fund loan or for overpayment of benefit. Sixty per cent said deductions made budgeting more difficult and 24 per cent say they make budgeting much worse. This is discussed below in more detail in the section on problems with direct payments.

Ensuring the payment of essentials over other debts or commitments

Direct payments prioritise payment for essentials such as fuel, water, and rent. A number of money advisers pointed out that it is so difficult to manage on a low income that an unexpected contingency will often become a higher priority than the payment for fuel, housing or water. Without direct payments, higher priority might have been given to consumer credit repayments, hire purchase or catalogue commitments, or door-to-door lenders. Such creditors are likely to be more pressing. When he first got into debt for gas payments, an unemployed man with wife and six children who was in debt to a 'loan shark' (a lender who provides cash with little security at very high interest rates) said:

> ...if you didn't have a direct payment, you've got the money in your pocket, somebody knocks on your door, and it's mostly women and they rabbit you to death, so you just pay them and get rid of them. (Mr F)

Mr F went on to say that he would have paid the 'loan shark' rather than the gas bill because he could wait to pay until he gets a red bill. A number of money advisers also suggested that the creditor who knocks on the door every two weeks immediately after benefit has been paid often becomes the priority creditor because of the personal contact. Other debts are attended to later.

Direct payments are cheaper than many other methods of payment

In order to pay the rent or some other essential, people might borrow money at high rates of interest and face tough recovery procedures. For example the 'loan shark' described by Mr F charged a total of £45 interest on a short-term loan of £100.

Paying for fuel by pre-payment meter is also more expensive than fuel direct, because of the additional standing charge. At a more mundane level, direct payments mean that such costs as bus fares, postage or postal order charges to pay bills are avoided; Chapter Five discusses the costs of direct payments in more detail. Although these are not large costs they could be significant for people on low incomes.

All of the money advisers interviewed mentioned that the flat rate of £2.20 per week for recovery of a debt within the direct payment schemes was valued by users. They knew how much was being deducted each week and it was felt that the amount set was more realistic than collection through budget schemes or pre-payment meters operated by the utilities. Within these latter arrangements repayment of the arrears can be set inappropriately high. An example is given by a lone parent who paid £2.15 a week for the arrears and £7 a week for current consumption of gas. When asked if this seemed about the right amount for her, she replied she was happy to know the bills were being paid. She was thankful to the DSS for this because she felt that if *she* had been paying rather than the 'social', the gas company would have asked for more from her.

Equalising bills over the year

Direct payments can help to spread the costs of consumption over the year particularly for fuel. Fuel consumption is high in winter but can be considerably lower in summer. In addition, gas companies often calculate repayment arrangements as a percentage of current consumption in recovering debt. This can substantially increase the amount to be paid in the winter.

Water is billed only twice a year and as for fuel direct payments can help to spread the cost.

Help with mobility and access problems

Some of those interviewed, particularly disabled people, pensioners, and those with mobility problems, mentioned that direct payments were a convenient method of payment. Bills are paid without having to go out to post letters or visit gas or electricity centres, or impose on someone else to make the payment.

> Yes it has helped me because, I'm in a wheelchair and you can't always get people to take you to pay it. (Ms E)

A slightly different point was made by Ms F, a pensioner with a direct payment for rent, who could not get out very much because of difficulty in walking. Without the direct payment she would have had to rely on her nephew but she would have worried about bills being paid properly and that he might be cheating her.

Mr B, an unemployed man with direct payments for gas and rent arrears, mentioned the distance to the rent payment point as a problem and that direct payments removed the need for him to travel. The local office had moved and this meant an extra three-mile journey to pay only £2 each week for rent arrears. Mr B acknowledged that a rent collector came round but sometimes he would not be at home.

> It was just a lot easier just to say right just stop it and just pay them direct.

To summarise, our findings show that people on direct payments do find them useful and this reflects the results of other studies (Rowlingson and Kempson, 1993; NACAB, 1993b). Very few wished to finish using direct payments and change to an alternative method of payment. Direct payments reduced people's worries about failing to clear debts and the resulting possibilities of homelessness, or disconnection from fuel and water supplies. Information from the survey showed that direct payments for gas, electricity and water had helped with budgeting. The help given by direct payments to disabled people and others with mobility problems was highlighted in the qualitative interviews. In the next section we consider the disadvantages.

Disadvantages of direct payments

Underlying many of the disadvantages of direct payments noted in the literature is a complex exercise in three-way communication. Direct payment schemes involve three parties, the consumer, the creditor and the Benefits Agency, and to operate successfully depend on communication and co-operation between them. The consumer relies on the Benefits Agency to make payments on time and to say what payments are being made. The creditor needs to know that the Agency will make the payments regularly in order to remove the need for further debt recovery measures. They also need to tell the consumer the state of their debt. The Benefits Agency needs to be told what payments are to be made and to be kept informed of any changes.

The literature contains a list of disadvantages and problems with the direct payment schemes:

- delays in making decisions, and in the refunding of overpayments and credits

- overpayments: deductions sometimes continue to be made after the debt has been cleared

- lack of knowledge about the exact amounts paid to third-party creditors and when the actual transfer of money from the DSS takes place. This is particularly important for direct payment of mortgage interest because the client is still responsible for informing the Benefits Agency of changes in interest rates although no longer directly responsible for payment.

- direct payments reduce the amount of money over which a recipient has control

- in some cases payments are not the choice of the consumer

- for those with multiple debts for necessities, the possibility of having a particular debt paid by direct payment is pre-determined by the scheme

- the priority for payment between different debts is determined by the system

- the amount of benefit left for day-to-day expenses

- access: direct payments are only available to those in arrears, apart from the payment of mortgage interest, and to those on Income Support. They are not available to all who would choose to have them.

- companies can refuse direct payments in favour of a pre-payment meter regardless of a customer's wishes, or whether a meter is appropriate for them. Because of this deductions are sometimes discontinued after change of address.

We will consider the evidence for each of the following disadvantages or problems in turn: lack of information; administrative mistakes and delays; lack of flexibility; level of remaining benefit; increased consumption; sanctions not avoided; lack of choice; access.

Lack of information

One of the disadvantages of direct payments is the lack of information given by the Benefits Agency about when payments are made, and by the creditor about how much of the arrears has been paid off. A number of respondents in the qualitative interviews reported that they did not know how much was deducted from their benefit for direct payments.

> I don't know how much they're taking off or how much they're paying and whatever. My money went down a fiver this week and I haven't got a clue why. (Ms C, single parent)

Ms C went on to say that even when the Benefits Agency did send a letter it was not clear or easy to understand just what the position was. She wanted to know more about what was going on because it was her money. The gas company do

> sort of tell you when the social paid; but they send you bills and the social haven't paid. They are always late paying the direct debit.

Mr E, a single man, thought the gas company should inform him about the state of his account, but since he started with direct payments he had heard nothing and said he had not had any letters to let him know how much he had cleared. He had been told that he would be informed when the debt was cleared, but felt that could take over a year and he would like to see how he was progressing in the meantime.

Some money advisers also thought that the information provided by the Benefits Agency was very sketchy. There was a general feeling that those with direct payments were not provided with good information about what the Agency are actually paying, and even when letters arrived in time, they were not very easy to understand.

Administrative delays and mistakes

To avoid disconnection and other sanctions bills must be paid in time. If the responsibility for paying bills is passed from the consumer to the Benefits Agency, it is important that this arrangement does not introduce any delays in payment which put the consumer at risk. Among the problems identified in the qualitative interviews were delays in payments from the Benefits Agency to creditors and delays in communication between the Agency and the consumer. An unemployed man with direct payments for gas and mortgage had letters threatening disconnection because payments had not been made to British Gas.

> *I then got a letter from the gas board about two months later saying they hadn't had any money from me, so I rang and said, well it's the DHSS is paying. Said well the DHSS hasn't paid us. I then eventually got in contact with the DHSS...this went on for months. (Mr D)*

A single parent with direct payments for gas and rent had a similar experience:

> *I got a letter threatening to have my gas cut off...this was last year, at some point when I first got on to the direct payments and they hadn't received any money at all for six months. And I 'phoned the gas board and they said they hadn't received the forms from the benefit office or anything. (Ms G)*

Ms G went on to say that this was a problem between the DSS and the gas company and that it was eventually sorted out satisfactorily.

The Joint Statement of Intent, a joint agreement signed by the DSS and the fuel and water companies now includes maximum response times for the Benefits Agency and the utilities. A similar arrangement exists for payment of Council Tax arrears. However, problems do arise when those with direct payments move house, particularly to the area of a different electricity or gas company. The Benefits Agency sometimes cannot continue direct payments when the new electricity or gas company is unwilling to accept direct payments.

The circumstances described above are examples of administrative delays and mistakes where payments were not being made even though the consumer had been told that they were. Mistakes with mortgage interest payments were mentioned by some money advisers, one of whom considered miscalculations of interest a common problem.

> *There are always problems with the way the DSS calculate the interest, very often we come across a lot of cases where the interest has been incorrectly calculated which obviously leads to problems and increases the arrears.*

A money adviser also reported problems with the system for mortgage direct, an example of the complex interaction of the three parties; the consumer, mortgage lender and the Benefits Agency. The MI12 form from the Benefits Agency is completed by the claimant who takes it to the mortgage lender who then refers it to the Agency. The money adviser reported cases where the forms had been completed and sent but had not been received. It was difficult to know whether the fault lay with the lender or the Benefits Agency. However, since the Benefits Agency generally closes a case after two weeks if a MI12 is not returned, no payments were made. In one particular case the adviser said the claimant had filled in the form in October, the building society had stamped it in November and the Benefits Agency discovered it after the adviser telephoned about three times in February.

> *So they had it sent to them but they had lost it. In the meantime his case had been filed away because they don't leave cases out more than two weeks.*

Lack of flexibility

If income is diverted at source, it is less easy to 'rob Peter to pay Paul' in the short-term or to juggle with commitments, and there is less cash-in-hand to pay for emergencies and unexpected expenses. While some of those with direct payments readily acknowledged that direct payments reduced flexibility, many were prepared to tolerate this as the price to be paid to clear debts and avoid sanctions. In particular, the combination of direct payments for gas and a pre-payment meter for electricity was mentioned favourably, because it allowed people to budget for large gas bills yet keep some flexibility in electricity payments.

Level of remaining benefit

Direct payments inevitably reduce people's cash flow. Even though a proportion of benefit income is diverted to pay essential bills, there was still concern from some people interviewed that not enough was left for other expenditure. Mr H, a single man, felt he was struggling – each fortnight he received £54 from which he had £30 pounds taken off in payments for gas, Community Charge and water.

Mr D, an unemployed man with two children, said that despite direct payments he still did not pay all the bills because there was just not enough money. He said they lived '*on a very meagre ration*'. However most of those interviewed felt that the deductions were justified because the bills were paid.

The qualitative interviews reveal the tension between the competing ideals of paying one's bills and of having sufficient cash to pay for day-to-day expenses. This tension was illustrated well by Ms C, a single parent, with direct payments for gas and water charges. She found it hard but was glad her gas and water were paid for. She would have liked to pay more by direct payments but at the same time was concerned that she would find it harder to survive.

In the survey, people with a direct payment or deduction were asked if they had enough left to live on after the deduction. As this question was only asked of those with deductions, it is not possible to compare their responses with people with no deductions. However, we can make comparisons (Table 4.2) between those with one deduction and those with two or more, which will give some indication of the effect of having deductions from benefit. This analysis encompasses all deductions from benefit including those for repayments of Social Fund loans or for overpayment, since for the claimant the cumulative effect of deductions determines how much money is left to live on.

Table 4.2   Percentage who felt they had enough left to live on by number of deductions

Enough to live on	Number of deductions				
	1 %	**2** %	**3** %	**4 or more** %	**Any** %
Yes	46	36	31	21*	40
Not quite	25	32	28	5*	26
No, definitely not	26	32	42	68	32
N	**194**	**63**	**36**	**19**	**312**

* Fewer than 10 cases in the cell

NB. Percentages may not sum to 100%, either because responses of 'don't know' are not presented, or due to rounding.

Table 4.2 shows that, of the 312 with one or more direct deductions, 40 per cent said they had enough to live on. By contrast, 58 per cent felt this was not the case: 32 per cent felt they definitely did not have enough, and 26 per cent felt they had *not quite* enough.

Not surprisingly people were more likely to feel that they did not have enough as the number of deductions from benefit increased. Forty-six per cent of those with only one deduction felt they had enough to live on but this fell to 31 per cent of those with three deductions. Conversely 68 per cent of those with four or more deductions said they definitely did not have enough to live on compared with 26 per cent of those with one deduction.

The survey respondents were also asked the average amount deducted from benefit. For the 210 respondents who provided information, the average weekly deduction was £8.81. Excluded from this average were direct payments for mortgage interest and data from those respondents who confused a direct payment for rent with Housing Benefit. On average, deductions amounted to 17 per cent of the Income Support paid, but the proportion varied from six per cent for those with deductions of £2 or less to 22 per cent for those with deductions of £10 to £15, and to 36 per cent for those with deductions of £15 to £30. The deductions formed a lower proportion of *total income*, three per cent on average, and ranged from one per cent for those with deductions of £2 or less to six per cent of those with deductions between £15 and £30.

Increased consumption

Some creditors, particularly the fuel companies, maintained that once people were on direct payments their consumption increased. An interview with the manager of an electricity company illustrates this view:

> *...we found that the fuel direct scheme was a licence to use whatever amount of electricity they wanted to...At least double, so that basically what happened was that the debt due to us increased when they joined the scheme, which was ridiculous. So if the customer's agreed to pay £8 a week for on-going plus, let's say £2.15 for arrears, they're actually using £16 pounds worth a week. So that after six or 12 months' time the debt got increasingly worse. So in those circumstances we had to write to the DSS and ask for a considerable increase in the payment. Often the claimant hasn't got enough income for the deduction, so they then come off the scheme and they are then in a worse state than they were originally.*

A respondent from the electricity company in area 2 also mentioned this issue: certain clients felt that because their electricity was being paid for and they have nothing to show them how much they are using, their consumption tends to increase. He had evidence of this when he dealt with debt collection in the area, but was not sure whether this was still the case now that fewer people have direct payments for electricity.

A similar problem was reported with direct payments for gas. The respondent for British Gas in area 1 also said that as soon as people go on direct payments he could guarantee their bill would be higher than it had ever been before. In his view this was because people think *'if I'm only going to pay five pounds I can burn as much gas as I like.'* He also commented that the direct payment scheme is not explained very well by the Benefits Agency. Those using direct payments should be told that if consumption increases so will payments and if it decreases then payments will decrease. He said that, *'people think it's forever five pounds irrespective of consumption levels.'*

An officer from the Benefits Agency office in area 2 also reported having to raise direct payments to cover increased current consumption:

> *I suspect there could be a tendency for [increased consumption]. Subconsciously they might think 'I'm not paying for this, I can have it on as long as I want'. I think some people forget that they're really paying out of their benefit.*

When asked if he had any figures to support this claim the respondent elaborated:

> *I'm not saying it's across the board by any means...I tell you one thing that might be a little bit of evidence. The gas or fuel boards review the arrears every so often, they read the meter and submit the new arrears figures to us. Now we can kick somebody off with, let's say, two or three hundred pounds arrears. We're taking a direct payment for that so it's £7.50 plus £2.20 a week. And then in about six months' time we get a revision from the gas board, because suddenly the arrears are six hundred or seven hundred pounds.*

This is a particular problem when deductions are for current consumption. Fuel boards estimate the deduction to be made to cover current use on the previous year's consumption. If this is an underestimate and people consume more they build up further arrears.

In contrast, none of those on direct payments who were interviewed said they used more fuel after going onto direct payments. Ms D, a single parent, was aware of the problem and had been told that *'you've still got to watch what you're using.'* Similarly, Mr A, a single man, said he did not use more gas since being on direct payments – he felt he did not use a lot of gas or electricity. Current consumption might be greater than that estimated by the fuel boards because the estimate is based on consumption at the same quarter of the previous year. Current recipients of Income Support now using direct payments might have been in work at that time and not needed to use so much fuel in the home. Thus their current consumption can be underestimated by the fuel boards.

The problem of increased consumption is discussed from the utilities' point of view in Chapter Six.

Sanctions not avoided

Although direct payment schemes were introduced to help people on Income Support avoid the sanctions of disconnection from the fuel supply or eviction from home, we have already seen that administrative delays can bring the threat of disconnection. Our in-depth interviews with people on direct payments, however, did not reveal any cases of people on direct payments who had been disconnected or evicted. Most of the information about this problem came from interviews with money-advice agencies. They reported that sanctions are not always avoided and gave various reasons, including increased arrears while on direct payments, and administrative mistakes and delays.

Some people are refused access to the schemes, because they have insufficient Income Support or because of some other rule. Clearly if such people are disconnected or evicted it is not directly a fault of the people administering the schemes, unless they are making incorrect decisions. However, since one of the aims of the schemes is to avoid extreme sanctions, it could be argued that the present structure of the schemes is not helping some people who are clearly in need. The rules for direct payment of mortgage interest dictate that only eligible interest is payable. Eligible interest might not cover some second mortgages, interest on accrued arrears, mortgages for certain home improvements or, from April 1993, on that part of the mortgage over £150,000 and, from April 1994, on that part over £125,000. Lenders were offered obligatory direct payments for mortgage on the understanding that they would not seek possession where the direct payments meet the mortgage interest due. In practice, according to a spokesperson from the DSS, many lenders do not seek repossession unless the arrears are very high or the full interest is not covered by the direct payment. NACAB is concerned that this situation might change when the housing market improves as their report on deductions from benefit shows:

> *Moreover it is becoming increasingly apparent that the potential advantage of the scheme to the claimant – the removal of the ultimate sanction of eviction – is not being realised. As the housing market picks up, a growing number of bureaux are reporting clients threatened with repossession despite the payment of mortgage interest direct. (NACAB, 1993b, page 47)*

Thus there is some evidence that direct payments do not always protect people from sanctions. Liaison with creditors in these cases could establish whether the problems arose through administrative delays or through creditors applying sanctions inappropriately.

Lack of choice

Direct payments can be initiated by an adjudication officer without the recipient's consent if it is deemed to be 'in the best interest of the family'. Local authorities must obtain a court order to retrieve Community Charge arrears, and if the order is awarded an arrangement can be made with the DSS for direct payment without the benefit recipient's consent. Direct payments can be imposed to clear unpaid fines. This is somewhat similar to the arrangement whereby payments for fines can be deducted from earnings. Direct payments are also compulsory for mortgage interest if there is an agreement with the lender.

It might be expected that people would object to having deductions taken from their benefit without their consent. However, the overall picture to emerge from our 45 qualitative interviews with people using direct payments was that lack of choice did not worry them. Even when imposed, direct payments were still liked for their positive contribution to clearing arrears and to household budgeting.

In our survey, people who reported that their direct payment was either imposed or the idea of a third party rather than their own, were asked if they were willing or unwilling participants in the relevant scheme. The results, shown in Table 4.3, largely bear out the finding from the qualitative interviews that lack of choice over whether to participate in a direct payment scheme was not an issue for most people. Having said that, it is notable that the most reluctance was shown by people having direct payments for mortgage interest payments. Of the 52 respondents who were asked the question, 16 (31 per cent, compared with 17 per cent for all direct payments) said they were not willing participants. This is similar to NACAB's finding (1993c) that some pensioners who had been paying their mortgage interest with no difficulty were not happy with losing this control over their finances when compulsory mortgage direct was introduced.

Table 4.3 Willingness to participate in direct payment schemes among respondents who did not initially request a direct payment

Type of direct payment	Willingness to participate				
	Very willing	Willing	Not very willing	Not at all willing	Total
Gas	13	13	5	0	31
Electricity	8	13	2	1	24
Water	9	17	5	1	32
Rent	49	29	3	2	83
Mortgage	17	19	8	8	52
Community Charge	22	48	7	10	87
Total N	**118**	**139**	**30**	**22**	**309**
Percentage	**38**	**45**	**10**	**7**	

Policy implications

This chapter has outlined the main advantages and disadvantages of direct payments from the consumers' point of view. The main message coming from our in-depth interviews is that users of the schemes find them helpful; they feel reassured to have arrears paid and threats of disconnection and other sanctions removed. Much of the literature on the schemes comes from advice agencies and concentrates on the difficulties with the schemes, but these need to be set alongside this basic advantage. In spite of having money deducted with no choice in some cases, and having less money in hand for other expenses, users still said they were glad to have direct payments. They were also reassured that payments for essentials were being met. The other aspect of the schemes which seems to be particularly valued is that they overcome problems associated with access and mobility. Those with poor health or difficulty in walking mentioned this, but others who would have had to travel to make payments were also aware of the advantage. The value of spreading payments over the year was highlighted by advice agencies but was not mentioned by users. This could be because advice agencies are called in to help with debts arising from high fuel bills, and they see direct payments as a way of helping in these circumstances.

The main disadvantages identified in the literature and in the interviews were lack of information, administrative delays and mistakes. These are products of a relatively complex system which depends on the co-operation of three, and sometimes four participants: the user, the Benefits Agency, the creditor and often an advice agency.

The lack of information links with another aspect of the schemes in that they are administered by the Benefits Agency as systems of last resort, and are not available to all recipients of Income Support. If they were an integral part of the benefit then publicity and information would be more widely available and the administrative system would be more automatic. As it is, direct payments are a special service and less routine. To run efficiently for the benefit of the users, the direct payment schemes need to provide clear, easily understood, and regular information on when payments have been made, and the amount of payments made. It is not clear that the Benefits Agency's undertaking to improve response times covers all of these information requirements adequately. There may be a case for people with direct payments to be reviewed on a more regular basis than others on Income Support. Although providing information about the amount of arrears remaining and the amounts deducted for current consumption is not its responsibility, the Benefits Agency could encourage creditors to communicate fully with those on direct payments in the interests of improving the service to them.

Our research suggests that for those on direct payments the security of regular repayments of debt and uninterrupted supplies of housing services, fuel and water, outweighs the reduced flexibility in budgeting, and any lack of choice about starting direct payments. The direct payment schemes have expanded to include a wider range of payments for water, Council Tax and compulsory mortgage interest. Further, repayments of Social Fund loans, unpaid fines and overpayments of benefit are also deducted from benefit. This means that a few had more than four deductions from benefit and this group was likely to feel that they did not have enough to live on after deductions.

Among those interviewed from gas and electricity companies and the Benefits Agency there was a view that people on direct payments were likely to consume more fuel when payments were deducted from benefit. Consumers, however, did not feel they used fuel indiscriminately and were aware that if their consumption rose they would have to pay more. How the estimates for current consumption are calculated might require closer investigation by the utilities. At present estimates for current consumption are based on consumption for the similar period in the previous year. If people have started claiming Income Support since that time, their fuel consumption could have risen because they are no longer in work and are having to heat the home more. Increased consumption can lead to the discontinuation of a direct payment if the amount to be deducted for current consumption is too high compared with the Income Support for which the recipient qualifies. Disconnection might result. The payment of mortgage direct is another area where creditor sanctions might not be avoided. The direct payment might not cover all the interest due to the lender for mortgages on improvements and other items, for example.

To summarise, the main policy implication emerging from this consumers' view of direct payments is that they should be continued. They are helpful and valued by claimants. Even if no improvement were possible this would be the case. However, some suggestions for improvement have been outlined above. Briefly these are: better, more easily understood and regular information to the user; more regular review of direct payments cases; availability of money advice; liaison with creditors to review cases where sanctions have been imposed despite direct payments and to ensure that sanctions are not applied inappropriately; review of the way current consumption estimates are prepared. These policy options involve both creditors and the Benefits Agency and are discussed further in Chapter Eight.

Chapter 5 Coming Off Direct Payments and Alternative Methods of Payment

Introduction

We have explored the experience of Income Support recipients when coming onto and using direct payments in earlier chapters. In this chapter we review the experience of people who come off direct payments and discuss the issues surrounding the use of alternatives methods of paying arrears and other expenses.

The chapter is divided into the following sections:

- why recipients come off direct payments
- the consequences for recipients who have come off direct payments
- possible alternatives to direct payments, and
- the views and experiences that recipients have of these alternatives.

Reasons for coming off direct payments

Direct payments are discontinued for three reasons. First, when all outstanding arrears have been repaid; secondly, when Income Support recipients have transferred to another form of benefit; and thirdly, when they come off benefit altogether. An adjudication officer does have an element of discretion over whether direct payments should continue when arrears have been cleared (discussed more fully in Chapter Seven) but for the second and third reasons, direct payments are terminated automatically even though arrears may be outstanding.

Although the reason for discontinuing a direct payment is included in notification letters, 12 (24 per cent) of the 51 recipients in the survey who had finished having direct payments said they did not know why direct payments stopped. While it is possible that some people will not have read their letters in full, it is also possible that the information provided in the form of a standard letter was not sufficiently clear and understandable.

Some respondents in the in-depth interviews disagreed with the decision to take them off direct payments. Of these, none were aware that they had a right of appeal to challenge the decision even though notification letters contain this information. This suggests that there is scope for improving the content and presentation of information about decisions and about appeal rights.

Consequences of coming off direct payments

The discontinuation of direct payments has a range of immediate consequences, both financial and psychological, for Income Support recipients. They must retake control of their finances and assume responsibility for specific items of household expenditure. They must also find alternative methods of payment and reorganise household budgeting to accommodate these changes.

Using both quantitative and qualitative data, we explored the attitudes of people to coming off direct payments and how they coped with household budgeting.

Attitudes to coming off direct payments

The in-depth interviews showed that people had widely contrasting views and attitudes towards coming off direct payments. Some were generally pleased that direct payments had ceased since this increased their available income. Some also appreciated the additional choice and control that they now had over personal budgeting.

> *I got a letter saying the rent payments would stop from such a date...I was glad when it did...there's more money for other things now you know.*
> *(Mr H, unemployed man)*

Some people were glad to come off direct payments for reasons unconnected with the schemes themselves but because they did not like being in debt *per se*. There was a belief, particularly common among pensioners, that one should live within one's means and that debt was to be avoided if at all possible.

> *I was happy when I was off it (direct payments for gas), put it that way, because I could pay my own way, because if I'd got the money to pay for it myself I would have done...I'm nearly seventy, so, I mean our age group, we've always had to fight, and on our own sort of thing, you know. And my mother's always taught the lesson – if you can't afford it, don't buy it. (Ms G, pensioner)*

Conversely, some people would have preferred to continue with direct payments because they helped reduce the strain and anxiety associated with budgeting on a low income. This was particularly true for those who had acknowledged that they had poor budgeting and money management skills.

> *Since I went off Income Support, school meals have stopped, dental treatment, glasses, prescriptions have stopped, but I'll have to start paying the rent, the poll tax...I prefer them to pay it because that's why I'm on invalidity because me nerves, 'cos I can't do with the hassle of it. So it would be better if they could pay for me, you know take it out of the money...because we're useless at paying bills, I'll be honest with you, that's why I prefer the DHSS pays, because they take it out of the money before I get it then don't they. (Mr I, disabled man)*

For some respondents the cessation of direct payments resulted in a period of uncertainty, when they were anxious and worried about how they would manage their future budgeting. One had been notified that direct payments would cease for rent arrears and Community Charge arrears and visited the local Citizens Advice Bureau to discuss the situation.

> *They just sent me a letter saying 'you're on Invalidity Benefit' and everything stopped, you know it caused a bit of a panic really, they could have put it a bit more plainly...Like this is what your getting, you might have to pay or whatever, we thought we'd have to pay £47 rent, full poll tax...Well they were helpful (Citizens Advice Bureau) they wrote everything down, broke it all down what I'd be getting, what we are paying out and I felt a lot better. (Mr I, disabled man)*

For other respondents, the transition to financial autonomy was a less anxious and worrying time. In particular those who had been contacted by a creditor to arrange another payment method were generally less apprehensive about the future.

How recipients manage

The in-depth interviews showed that some people did manage to budget for household expenses after coming off direct payments, though not always without difficulty. Others found they could not manage, experienced considerable financial problems and defaulted on payments.

An unemployed single man explained that he had set up a budget account with the council to pay his rent arrears and he was currently adhering to these payments.

> *I've not got no arrears at the present for the rent...you see I've got this arrangement with the council that I go in and pay them every week, that way I don't get in trouble again, you see or I might spend it on other things. (Mr J)*

Another unemployed single man explained that after coming off direct payments for gas arrears, he was managing to budget with the aid of a pre-payment meter.

> *They deduct it now through the actual gas meter itself...I can balance everything out during the week, you know I can say well I can use five pounds worth of gas*

every week...then I haven't got to worry about a big bill coming at the end of the quarter...It's so convenient now, I mean all I have to do, like when I get my giro now I just go up to the post office, get a pound of gas. (Mr K, unemployed man)

Some people reported that the Benefits Agency had not notified them that direct payments had stopped. One man had incurred further gas arrears in this way and was currently applying to go back on to direct payments.

They told me nothing about it stopping...The first thing I knew was when we got the bill for the gas and we owed them money. Well I couldn't manage it after the 'social' stopped paying. I kept saying I would put a bit to one side to pay the gas. But I didn't and got in a mess again. I'm trying again to let the 'social' pay it for me. (Mr N, unemployed man)

We found no clear link between how people managed when they came off direct payments and the original cause of their debt. Currently, there are no large-scale data on the proportion of people who get into financial difficulties once direct payments have finished, or how long they manage before the onset of difficulties. Evidence from other related research suggests that budget agreements are often broken after an initial 'honeymoon' period when payments are maintained. Mannion (1992) found that the 'honeymoon' period during which arrears payments for consumer credit and fuel are adhered to typically lasts between six and nine months. After this period a high proportion of payments cease to be made.

Alternatives to direct payments

The Benefits Agency provides direct payments as a service of 'last resort'. Such a policy necessarily relies on judgements about the financial and social welfare implications of alternative payment methods. Only when alternative payment methods are regarded as inappropriate or impractical do adjudication officers consider direct payments as an option.

Although direct payments may be useful to people, it is important to assess whether and how they would have coped if direct payments did not exist. Arguments to phase out, or restrict direct payments may be stronger if it is shown that many people can manage their own budgeting in their absence. Alternatively, if people are not able to cope, there might be a case for expanding the availability of direct payment schemes.

How recipients said they would have coped without direct payments

Evidence from our research suggests that many Income Support recipients would not have been able to manage their financial affairs without direct payments, and would have accrued larger arrears in their absence.

In the questionnaire survey we asked respondents how they would have managed to pay for financial commitments covered by direct payments, if direct payments did not exist. Table 5.1 presents their responses.

According to the responses, 39 per cent of bills for fuel, water and housing costs would not have been paid. We can also interpret these figures as supporting the usefulness of direct payments to people. The responses indicate that a large proportion of people currently on direct payments might have been subject to creditor sanctions such as disconnection and eviction if direct payments had not been available. However, since non-payment is only a temporary solution unless the consumer is willing to face eviction or disconnection, it is likely that most of these people would eventually find a way to meet their financial commitments. For 22 per cent of direct payments, respondents said they did not know what they would do in their absence. This could reflect a widespread ignorance of the availability of alternative payment methods.

Table 5.1 How recipients would have managed in the absence of direct payments+

	Gas	Electricity	Water	Rent	Mortgage	Community Charge	All
	%	%	%	%	%	%	%
Not paid	48	52	30	30	14*	57	39
Spent it	–	–	–	10	3*	3*	4
Struggled/borrowed	9*	19*	20	11	14*	7*	12
Cut off/evicted	11	4*	2*	1*	2*	–	3
Managed/saved/used budget scheme	9*	24*	8*	12	36	9	14
Other	4*	–	2*	11	8*	5*	6
Don't know	19	–	38	26	24	18	22
N	54	21	50	103	59	110	397

+ percentages represent direct payments, not numbers of people
* based on fewer than 10 cases
Source: Questionnaire Survey

The in-depth interviews also suggest that some people would have struggled to meet financial commitments or defaulted on payment.

> *I don't think I would have coped or I'd have been struggling in trying to pay it (gas bill) and it would worry me. (Ms C, single parent)*

> *I'd struggle again (to pay rent) and get in more debt again, which I'm bound to do I mean I'm having it stopped now and I can't touch it so that way I know I've got a roof over my head – otherwise I'm not going to have a roof over my head. (Mr B, unemployed man)*

Similarly, some respondents stated that they did not know how they would have managed if they had not used direct payments.

> *I just don't know what we'd have done thinking about it...There's not a lot you can do when they're coming to cut you off. (Mr E, unemployed man)*

Table 5.1 also shows that survey respondents said that they would have managed, saved or used a budget scheme for 14 per cent of direct payments and thought they would have struggled or borrowed to pay a further 12 per cent. This suggests that possibly a quarter of people would have been able to meet their financial commitments in some way in the absence of direct payments.

The reported ability or willingness to meet financial commitments varied by the type of direct payment made. In the survey we found that many Community Charge payments in particular would not have been paid, and gas and electricity payments were less likely to have been paid than water and rent. As shown in Chapter Three, opposition to the Community Charge might contribute to the higher proportion reporting they would not pay the tax. It could also indicate that money allocated for the Community Charge is a 'soft target' when money is needed for something else. Moreover, it may also suggest that direct payments for the Community Charge are possibly the only effective method of getting some Income Support recipients to pay the tax. We show in Chapter Six that this opinion is held by some local authority staff.

Conversely, many mortgage interest payments would have been paid by budget schemes or other managing strategies. In the absence of direct payments, recipients would be paid the full eligible mortgage interest element as part of the Income Support payment. In this situation it may be easier for respondents to envisage that they could meet mortgage payments.

It is also striking that for over a third of water payments, recipients reported that they did not know what they would do. This may reflect a lack of information provided by water companies about alternative methods available to pay for water charges.

Implications for refused applicants

Recipients who are refused direct payments have to continue with existing methods of payment or find an alternative.

Of the six unsuccessful applications for direct payments by respondents in the qualitative interviews, four were for gas, one for electricity and one for water charges. None of these people had been subject to creditor sanctions. Three were managing to reduce their arrears, two had set up a budget account with British Gas and the other had arranged an instalment plan with the water company. Of the three who were not reducing their arrears, one was considering purposefully withholding payments to British Gas so that she could accrue sufficient arrears to be considered for direct payments. The other two were in the process of having pre-payment meters installed which would be calibrated to recover a proportion of arrears.

Hence, of the six respondents refused direct payments, five were reducing or about to reduce their arrears. The findings seem to vindicate the decision by the adjudication officer, since all of them were able to find alternative payment methods and none was subject to creditor sanctions. The respondent not paying her gas bill so that she could accrue large enough arrears to be considered for direct payments, highlights a perverse incentive that exists for people to get into debt.

Payment methods used by Income Support recipients

Previous studies (Berthoud and Kempson, 1992; Parker, 1990; Mannion, 1992) show that low-income households are often faced with more restricted choice of payment methods than those on higher incomes and hence incur additional costs. For example, pre-payment meters for fuel have higher standing charges and tariffs than other methods of paying for fuel, and customers may incur additional travel costs associated with obtaining tokens or recharging cards.

Our survey reveals that many Income Support recipients are effectively denied the option of paying by standing order and direct debit, two of the cheapest methods. We found that fewer than half (49 per cent) have a bank or building society account. (This figure is similar to the Berthoud and Kempson survey which found that half of non-pensioner households with a weekly income of less than £100 had no bank account and that only one in ten had an account with an overdraft facility.)

In the rest of this section we focus on the alternative methods used by Income Support recipients to pay for fuel and assess the implications for them of alternative methods.

Electricity

Almost half (49 per cent) of our survey respondents paid for their electricity quarterly in arrears by direct debit, cash or cheque (Table 5.2). Almost a third used a pre-payment meter, 15 per cent a budget account and only one per cent had direct payments. The relatively high number of people paying by pre-payment meter compared with direct payments, reflects the policy of many electricity companies to accept direct payments only where a pre-payment meter is not considered practical. The following chapter discusses this practice in more detail.

Methods used to pay for electricity differed markedly between claimant groups. Over two-thirds of pensioners (68 per cent) paid for their electricity by cash or cheque, compared with approximately one in five (21 per cent) of lone parents. It is striking that only six per cent of pensioners reported that they used a pre-payment meter to pay for electricity. This compares with over half (51 per cent) of lone parents and more than a third of unemployed people.

Table 5.2 Methods of paying for electricity by claimant group

Method of payment	Unemployed	Lone parents	Pensioners	Disabled	Other	All
	%	%	%	%	%	%
Direct debit	4	5	5	9	5	5
Cash/cheque	38	21	68	39	36	44
Direct payment	1	3	1	3	–	1
Pre-payment meter	38	51	6	31	45	30
Budget scheme	15	17	15	14	7	15
Stamps	1	2	3	2	2	2
Paid with rent	3	1	2	2	5	2
Other	–	–	–	–	–	–
Don't know	–	–	–	–	–	–
N	287	200	300	96	42	925

Source: Questionnaire Survey

Gas

Over three-quarters (78 per cent) of Income Support recipients in the survey paid for their gas quarterly in arrears, by direct debit, cash or cheque (Table 5.3). One in ten paid by a pre-payment meter, five per cent by direct payment and a similar number by a budget scheme.

Pensioners' methods of paying for gas differed from other claimant groups. They were less likely than others to pay by direct debit or use a pre-payment meter and more likely to pay by cash or cheque.

Table 5.3 Methods of paying for gas by claimant group

Method of payment	Unemployed	Lone parents	Pensioners	Disabled	Other	All
	%	%	%	%	%	%
Direct debit	11	8	6	14	10	8
Cash/cheque	66	63	84	54	65	70
Direct payment	5	11	3	8	–	5
Pre-payment meter	13	9	1	14	15	10
Stamps	2	–	1	–	–	–
Paid with rent	2	–	–	–	–	–
Budget scheme	2	8	–	6	5	4
Don't know	2	1	5	4	5	3
N	122	85	140	50	20	417

Source: Questionnaire Survey

Having outlined the alternative payment methods used by Income Support recipients to pay for fuel, we now consider the two most common alternative payment methods offered to those experiencing difficulties paying for fuel: pre-payment meters and budget schemes.

Pre-payment meters

Almost a third (30 per cent) of survey respondents used a pre-payment meter to pay for their electricity, and one in ten did so for gas. The majority of respondents who used a pre-payment meter to pay for electricity (82 per cent) and gas (80 per cent), positively chose this method of payment.

The in-depth interviews showed that the respondents had varying attitudes towards pre-payment meters. Some were vehemently opposed to using them whereas others were strong supporters. Although many respondents reported problems with the day-to-day use of pre-payment meters, generally we found that those actually using them preferred this method of payment.

There were a number of reasons why people favoured pre-payment meters. First, they prevent arrears because it is not possible to obtain credit from them (apart from emergency credit in the case of electricity meters). For some recipients this is an important feature because it takes away the strain and anxiety associated with having to budget for fuel bills of an unknown size.

We know that we've got no big bills to manage when they come in and we use only what we can afford. Before we were getting into debt because you can't always pay for what you've used...There's less pressure with the meter because you've got no red bills coming through your letter box. (Mr K, unemployed man)

Secondly, pre-payment meters allow recipients to regulate and monitor their fuel consumption. This can promote energy awareness and help people to prioritise their use of fuel.

Well I've worked it out right to the fraction...I know exactly how much I put in. I've worked it out to a fine art that I know exactly what I would get to a pound...By just using the electric normal, checking it on the clock face and then when 24 hours has gone by having a look at it again and dividing it up into a pound I know it. (Mr E, unemployed man)

Thirdly, pre-payment meters can provide a form of saving since rebates can be paid when meters are emptied or recalibrated. This can be important for those households who do not have bank and building society accounts.

The electric's good...every so often I get a rebate back which helps to pay for something else. (Mr A, unemployed man)

Finally, pre-payment meters may be preferred because they allow more short-term financial flexibility than direct payments. People with pre-payment meters have the opportunity to 'rob Peter to pay Paul' by using money which is normally devoted to pay for fuel consumption to pay for contingencies that may assume greater importance in the short-term.

Both our qualitative and quantitative research shows that pre-payment meters can cause a number of problems. First, they allow the possibility of 'self-disconnection'. This can occur because people choose to use less fuel, cannot afford to feed the meter, or cannot access token outlets and recharging sites. These disconnections are also 'hidden' in the sense that outside bodies, for instance social services departments, do not know that a home is without fuel.

The survey found that almost a third of pre-payment meter users for gas (30 per cent) and over a third (36 per cent) of pre-payment meter users for electricity said they had wanted to use fuel during the previous month (January or February 1993) but were unable to. Most of these, 92 per cent of electricity meter users and 81 per cent of gas meter users, reported that this was due to not having enough money. Others did not use their meters because of problems with recharging keys or buying tokens. Of the 47 recipients who reported that they had been in the situation of wanting to use fuel, but could not, 18 were lone parents, four were pensioners, eight were unemployed with children under 5, and one was disabled. Many of these people who had self-disconnected would have been protected by the fuel companies' codes of practice from having their fuel supply disconnected if they had used a credit meter. However, customers with pre-payment meters are not protected by this code. This suggests that the use of pre-payment meters could carry risks for some people, particularly in the most vulnerable groups, which credit meters would prevent.

The survey also showed that the amount of time it took for people to travel to obtain tokens or recharge keys varied. For almost two-thirds (63 per cent) the average travelling time was less than 15 minutes, and for almost a quarter (23 per cent) journeys took more than 30 minutes.

Many respondents in the in-depth interviews reported that they had problems getting to token dispensers and key recharging points. Some had difficulties travelling to dispensers or problems getting access to them when outlets selling tokens were closed.

The only problems that they have is that, with the tokens is the post office down here, where everyone goes they don't sell em...or else you've got to get to the other side of town...Well I think they should have a machine so that you can get them any time that you want. (Ms G, single parent)

We also found, however, that self-disconnection did not always incline people towards direct payments. Some respondents preferred pre-payment meters even though they frequently went without fuel.

What's good about the electric though is if you haven't got the money you can't run it and that's the end of subject...I mean we spent many a time with no gas, no heating. (Mr K, unemployed man)

Another respondent reported that he preferred a pre-payment meter for electricity, even though he frequently ran out of money towards the end of the week.

I'd sooner pay it by key...Well if I put it in on the Monday, I put the key in six, seven pound, that runs somewhere out about Sunday you know. So you'll get over Sunday until the following Monday. (Mr B, unemployed man)

Some respondents had previously used pre-payment meters, but because of the inconvenience and the possibility of self-disconnection preferred direct payments. An unemployed man explained why he preferred direct payments to a pre-payment meter for gas:

No way do I want one again (pre-payment meter)...With the 'social' paying you know you always can have the heating on if you want it on...there's no hassle this way about running and borrowing after money all the time to pay the meter...and not having it on if you haven't got any. (Mr D, unemployed man)

Overall we found that people generally preferred pre-payment meters for electricity rather than for gas. Electricity pre-payment meters allow emergency credit and can be calibrated so that arrears are repaid on a weekly basis rather than as a proportion of current consumption. Gas pre-payment meters on the other hand do not offer emergency credit facilities and recover arrears as a proportion of consumption. This means that consumers pay more arrears off in winter than summer months and can, as a result, experience problems when heating is most needed.

For some people the financial and social welfare costs of pre-payment meters can be high. Our research shows that some households do 'self-disconnect' and are left with no lighting or heating. All meter users will incur additional costs associated with higher tariffs, recharging cards or obtaining tokens. These findings reflect those of previous research (Birmingham Settlement *et al.*, 1993) which also shows that families sometimes self-disconnect and incur higher costs associated with pre-payment meters.

Budget schemes

As we have shown earlier, one in seven of the survey respondents paying for electricity and four per cent paying for gas used a budget account with payments made weekly, fortnightly or monthly. Budget schemes have a number of advantages. First, they allow payments to be spread evenly throughout the year even though fuel consumption may vary. Secondly, they can aid budgeting by scheduling payments so that they match the timing of benefit payments. Finally, budget schemes allow more short-term financial flexibility than direct payments since payments can often be delayed for a few days if a person needs money to pay for other contingencies.

The in-depth interviews showed, however, that some people find it very difficult to maintain payments for budget schemes because they spend the money on other items.

Well they offered me a payment plan (gas) which I tried, but I mean if you're on a low income anyway and you need something it's easier to spend the money than it is to hand it over for the gas, which is wrong, but that's what you do.
(Mr G, lone parent)

Failure to comply with budget agreements may subject users to creditor sanctions. We found that many of the recipients in the qualitative interviews had failed to keep to budget payments prior to using direct payments.

Summary and policy implications

In this chapter we have shown that although for some Income Support recipients, the transition from direct payments to financial autonomy is a time of anxiety and worry, for most it is a relatively painless process. Whereas people do not always experience financial problems after coming off direct payments, some do and get into further financial difficulties. From our small qualitative sample we found no clear link between the reasons why people originally get into debt and how they fared when they came off direct payments. In the experience of the Benefits Agency and third-party creditors (see Chapter Six and Chapter Seven) many people will default on payment and will again be put on to direct payments.

Our discussion of the available alternatives to direct payments has shown their value to some people. Direct payments offer a unique service that is not provided by alternative methods of payment. Unlike pre-payment meters for instance, they guarantee that homes will have light and heat, and consumers are not inconvenienced by having to travel to recharge keys/cards or buy tokens. Unlike budget schemes, direct payments guarantee that payments are made and also prioritise housing and essential utility supplies above other short-term draws on income. Nevertheless we have also shown that some people prefer alternative methods of payment to direct payments. Their choice may depend as much on personal taste and preference as on household circumstances or the policies of third parties. Pre-payment meters, for instance, allow recipients to avoid debt and regulate energy consumption. Budget accounts can offer short-term financial flexibility not possible under direct payments.

Many Income Support recipients find direct payments a useful and convenient method of payment. However, the majority are also taken off a scheme once their arrears have been paid although some will wish to continue with direct payments. A policy option open to the DSS which would improve and extend its customer service would be to offer to people the opportunity of continuing to use a direct payment to pay for current consumption. This extension of choice would be in keeping with the spirit of the Citizen's Charter but would also increase the administrative costs of the Benefits Agency. However, some of these costs would be offset against the costs associated with closing down and restarting direct payments.

No one in our study knew that they had a right of appeal against an adjudication officer's decision to refuse direct payments. Some Benefits Agency staff were also not sure whether recipients were notified of their rights of appeal. There is however a statutory duty to inform anyone receiving an adjudication officer's decision of their rights of appeal. It is possible that some recipients would want to appeal if they knew they could. A review of the content and presentation of information about appeal rights would, therefore, appear justified.

Because of the administrative costs of setting up a direct payment, the Benefits Agency has an interest in reducing the number of people who, having come off a scheme, accrue arrears and return to direct payments. Previous research (Mannion, 1992) has shown that money advice services are often an effective method of preventing people returning to debt. In the light of this, both the Benefits Agency and creditors could benefit from the more widespread use of these services by Income Support recipients. This could be achieved in a number of ways. First, the Benefits Agency and creditors could publicise the availability of money advice agencies. Information could be targeted, for instance, at people who are about to be taken off direct payments, perhaps a month or two in advance. This would give people the opportunity to seek advice about budgeting and the most appropriate payment methods for them. Secondly, the Benefits Agency could provide an 'aftercare' service, such as a helpline, to offer advice and information to people who have come off, or are about to come off a direct payment scheme. Any additional costs incurred by the Benefits Agency in extending customer service by providing limited money advice directly would be partially offset by a reduction in the numbers of Income Support recipients who return to direct payments later.

In this chapter we have examined the experience of Income Support recipients when coming off direct payments and discussed the issues surrounding the possible alternatives for direct payments. In the following chapter we examine these issues from the perspective of third-party creditors and discuss their policies regarding direct payments.

Chapter 6   Third-Party Creditor Perspectives[3]

Introduction

For direct payment schemes to be successful in safeguarding housing and essential utility supplies, the Benefits Agency must secure the co-operation of third-party creditors who are paid directly. It is important therefore to appreciate the reasons why creditors agree to direct payment schemes, or alternatively, prefer other methods of payment and arrears recovery, to identify any problems or difficulties that they experience with direct payment schemes and consider views regarding how the service could be improved.

Our principal approach to identifying the views and practices of creditors about direct payment schemes was to gather information from people involved in their operation. We obtained information from senior and middle managers at the headquarters and five regions of British Gas; six regional electricity companies; five water companies; 15 local authorities concerning rent arrears; and ten local authorities concerning Community Charge arrears. In addition we also spoke to staff from the utility regulators, OFGAS, OFFER, OFWAT, the Gas Consumers Council, the Water Services Association and the Council for Mortgage Lenders (CML).

This chapter focuses on the views of third-party creditors. The views of Benefits Agency staff are detailed in the next chapter. We discuss, for each third party, current figures on arrears and enforcement proceedings; policy and staff attitudes towards direct payments; administrative problems associated with the schemes; and views about how the service could be improved.

Mortgage lenders

Number of direct payments

Income Support for mortgage interest has increased significantly over recent years. In 1992–93, £1,143 million was provided for mortgage interest. This represents almost a four-fold increase on the £286 million provided in 1988–89 (CML, 1993). In November 1992 over half a million Income Support recipients had mortgage interest payments included in their weekly assessments (Table 6.1). For those whose payments were met in full, the average weekly amount was £47.30.

Table 6.1   Number of claimants with allowances for mortgage interest, and average weekly amounts of awards

	ASE May 1990	ASE May 1991	ASE May 1992	QSE November 1992
Number of claimants ('000s)				
Half mortgage interest	40	73	64	70
Full mortgage interest	270	337	337	466
Total N	**310**	**410**	**499**	**536**
Average weekly amount (£)				
Half mortgage interest	33.69	35.61	30.26	28.08
Full mortgage interest	34.42	46.34	46.07	47.30

Source: DSS Annual Statistical Enquiry (ASE) and Quarterly Statistical Enquiry (QSE), 1993

3 Third-party creditors include local authorities, mortgage lenders, fuel and water companies.

LIVERPOOL JOHN MOORES UNIVERSITY
LEARNING SERVICES

Mortgage arrears and repossessions

Mortgage arrears rose sharply between 1989 and 1992. Over this period the number of cases between six and 12 months in arrears increased more than three-fold and the number of cases with arrears of 12 months or more increased more than ten-fold. Similarly, the number of home repossessions more than quadrupled between 1989 and 1992, from under 16,000 to almost 70,000 per year (Table 6.2). Recently, however, published statistics show that this trend is reversing with both the number of repossessed properties and the overall number of loans in serious arrears beginning to fall, although the number of loans 12 months or more in arrears are showing a slight increase (CML, 1993). The Council for Mortgage Lenders attributes the recent fall in repossessions to the beneficial impact of the introduction of direct payments for mortgage interest as well as a more favourable economic climate, particularly recent reductions in interest rates and the downward trend in unemployment (CML, 1993). Recent research (Ford, 1993), estimates that 17 per cent of Income Support recipients having mortgage direct are in arrears to lenders.

Table 6.2 Mortgage arrears (of six months and more) and repossessions 1989–1992

Year	Number of mortgages at year end	Repossessions during year	Cases in mortgage arrears	
			6–12 months	12+ months
1989	9,125,000	15,810	66,800	13,840
1990	9,415,000	43,890	123,110	36,100
1991	9,815,000	75,540	183,610	91,740
1992	9,922,000	68,540	205,010	147,040
1993	10,137,000	58,540	164,620	151,810

Source: CML, 1993

Policy and attitudes towards direct payments

Most mortgage lenders are supporters of direct payments. This is reflected in the large proportion of lenders who have opted to be included in the scheme. Currently, approximately 700 out of 900 lenders are paid direct. Indeed the Council for Mortgage Lenders actively campaigned for the introduction of compulsory direct payments for borrowers who are eligible for Income Support. Mortgage lenders are charged for the direct payments service at £1 per transaction. Some lenders feel that a charge should be made only where individual direct payments are above a certain level. Otherwise the direct payments may not be cost-effective as the £1 administration charge could be high compared with the level of payment for mortgage interest. At present lenders opting to use the scheme must include all their eligible customers for direct payments and pay the same transaction costs for all levels of direct payment.

The Council for Mortgage Lenders estimates that the financial benefits of direct payments to mortgage lenders are substantial. In December 1991, a selection of CML members were asked by the CML for their estimates of how much Income Support for mortgage interest received by their borrowers was actually paid to lenders. The highest estimate was 80 per cent and the lowest 25 per cent, with most of the estimates around 50 per cent. If only half of the money received by recipients was paid to borrowers, this would have represented a shortfall of £475.5 million in the financial year 1991–92. As lenders did not originally know which of their borrowers were receiving Income Support, it is difficult to establish precisely the size of the shortfall and therefore these figures should be interpreted with caution.

Mortgage lenders have over recent years extended the range of services available to borrowers experiencing repayment difficulties. Recovery and payment strategies for those in arrears now include deferred interest and suspension of payments; capitalisation of arrears; lower, monthly payments; extended mortgage terms; transfer to another form of mortgage; and interest-only payments. In some circumstances, lenders will also advise borrowers to sell their property. A recent study by the National Consumer Council (NCC, 1992) found that four-fifths of building societies used the interest-only option and approximately two-thirds made use of extending mortgage terms and lowering monthly payments. By contrast, fewer than 15 per cent of building societies would defer interest payments, and only slightly more than a third of building societies were willing to consider capitalising the arrears. Around a third were willing to recommend that the borrower sold the property, although many stressed that this was a last resort and only suggested in a small number of cases. Non-building society lenders were found to offer a more restricted range of debt recovery strategies.

In the absence of direct payments, the main problems for lenders, according to the CML, would be recovering all the money due to them, and identifying those borrowers who were receiving Income Support. In this situation lenders would have to ask borrowers whose accounts were in arrears if they were receiving Income Support and make the appropriate payment arrangements.

The CML also think that any future increase in house prices and the consequential reduction in the level of negative equity would not incline lenders to seek more repossessions, even where direct payments did not cover the full mortgage amount. Having spent time and resources looking at how they can help people who have problems, it was thought that lenders were unlikely to abandon this approach in favour of increasing repossession proceedings. Recent reports, however, (NACAB, 1993a; NACAB, 1993b) detail a number of cases where lenders have sought possession when Income Support recipients were only having part of their mortgage interest paid by the Benefits Agency.

Administration of direct payments

A number of administrative problems surround the direct payment scheme for mortgage interest. The CML report that these problems have been the subject of discussions with the DSS and that lenders are working closely with the Benefits Agency to overcome and find solutions to these problems. The seven principal problems associated with the scheme are outlined below.

- The CML are concerned about the administrative burden placed upon lenders since the introduction of direct payments. Of particular concern is the amount of time spent by staff completing the MI12 and MI12R forms used to adjudicate applications for direct payments. Some lenders have had to set up specific administrative units to deal with the additional workload. The CML are currently working closely with the Benefits Agency to simplify these forms.

- The CML report that lenders would appreciate earlier notification from the Benefits Agency about decisions to grant Income Support for mortgage interest to borrowers. Lenders are concerned that arrears can build up while they are waiting for notification. The CML has pressed the DSS for notification of Income Support decisions, particularly for those customers who are already in arrears, but this has not been possible for reasons of confidentiality.

- The CML believe that there is a lack of reciprocity between local Benefits Agency offices and lenders concerning the disclosure of information about recipients. Whereas the CML believe that lenders are very willing to divulge information about borrowers, they perceive that the Benefits Agency do not return this service. In particular, lenders are often frustrated when requesting information about a person's household circumstances and income to update their records. Lenders recognise that the Benefits Agency has a duty of confidentiality in respect of personal data, and therefore certain information may not be disclosed. However, the CML thought that there needs to be a better balance between the information exchanged between the two parties.

- The CML argue that variation in the application and payment procedures used by local Benefits Agency offices can cause administrative problems for lenders. The CML reported that after discussion with the DSS, the Agency is producing a standard document for the administration of direct payments which, it is hoped, will help promote a more consistent service from their offices.

- The CML report that some payments were not actually made by the Benefits Agency via the bankers automated clearing system (BACS). They saw

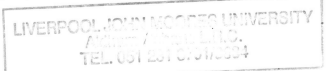LIVERPOOL JOHN MOORES UNIVERSITY
TEL. 051 231 3701/3634

55

administrative errors such as attaching incorrect account numbers to payments by the Benefits Agency as the main cause of the problem. As a result, lenders sometimes experienced lengthy delays awaiting the correction of these mistakes and incurred additional administration costs. Concern was also expressed that this subjected some people to undue worry. The CML thought the computerisation of direct payments for mortgage interest has largely overcome these difficulties.

- The CML were concerned that direct payments paid to lenders four weeks in arrears do not correspond with conventional calendar-monthly mortgage payments. Some recipients will technically fall into arrears as lenders receive 13 payments instead of 12 calendar-month payments over a year. The CML reported that lenders would not normally charge borrowers for the arrears that arise due to payments paid on a four-weekly basis.

- Problems are caused when Income Support recipients do not inform the Benefits Agency of interest rate changes. This can result in additional administration for lenders and the Benefits Agency who have to rectify under or overpayments. Although it is currently the responsibility of the borrower to provide notification of interest rate changes, lenders are at present working with the Benefits Agency to see whether there is a practical way for all lenders to do this.

In summary, most mortgage lenders wish to participate in the direct payment scheme because they view it as a cost-effective method of receiving payments from borrowers in receipt of Income Support. However, lenders have had to take on a large, additional workload caused by direct payments and have experienced a number of administrative problems. This discussion has focused on the views of the Council of Mortgage Lenders. In the following chapter we detail a number of problems identified by Benefits Agency staff relating to how lenders administer direct payments. Lenders are currently working closely with the DSS and the Benefits Agency to resolve these problems.

Local authorities

Local authorities principally receive direct payments for rent arrears and Community Charge arrears, although some councils also receive direct payments for water and fuel charges, mortgage interest, and residential care home and nursing home charges. Direct payments for rent arrears and Community Charge arrears are usually processed by housing departments and by treasurers' departments respectively.

Rent arrears:

Number of direct payments for rent arrears

In May 1992, 85,000 Income Support recipients had direct payments for rent arrears and amenity charges.

Number and size of arrears

In March 1992, over 40 per cent of council tenants (1.6 million people) were not fully up to date with their rent (Table 6.3). Almost three-quarters of tenants in arrears owed less than 13 weeks rent, and less than one in five of those with arrears owed more than the equivalent of 26 weeks rent.

Table 6.3 Size of local authority rent arrears at March 1992

	Number of tenants	Percentage of all tenants
Average by length of arrears		
<13 weeks	1,190,000	30.0
13–26 weeks	143,000	3.6
>26 weeks	268,000	6.7
Arrears by amount		
<£100	1,012,000	25.5
£100–£500	422,000	10.6
>£500	167,000	4.2
Total tenants in arrears	**1,601,000**	**40.3**

Source: CIPFA, 1993

The number of tenants in arrears and amounts of arrears vary by type of authority. In March 1992 the average amount owed in arrears by current tenants in metropolitan districts was £279, compared with only £134 in non-metropolitan districts (Table 6.4). Similarly the amount owed by former tenants was larger in metropolitan districts than non-metropolitan districts.

Table 6.4 Local authorities arrears statistics at March 1992

Analysis of arrears and amounts written off			Metropolitan districts	Non-Metropolitan districts	All authorities
Total sum due		£m	3,082.5	3,210.0	6,292.5
Income	Housing Benefit	£m	1,646.8	1,560.7	3,207.5
	Direct from tenant	£m	1,424.7	1,635.4	3,060.1
Amounts written off	Current tenants	£m	5.5	1.1	6.6
	Former tenants	£m	25.7	12.7	37.4
Former tenants' arrears	Number		231,464	148,045	379,509
	Amount	£m	103.0	35.1	138.1
	Average	£	445	237	364
Current tenants' arrears	Number		860,373	740,684	1,601,057
	Amount	£m	240.3	99.5	339.8
	Average	£	279	134	212
Total in arrears		%	**46.0**	**35.3**	**40.3**

Source: CIPFA, 1993

On the basis of their representative survey, Berthoud and Kempson (1992) estimated that more than one million tenants (18 per cent of the total) faced problems with rent arrears over the course of a year. For households in their survey rent accounted for only four per cent of all commitments, but 22 per cent of all debts. The Berthoud and Kempson survey found that the overwhelming majority (95 per cent) of households with rent arrears were living in local authority housing, with rent arrears relatively rare among private tenants.

Policy and attitudes toward direct payments for rent arrears

Our research shows that direct payments are viewed by many councils as an important if not indispensable method of rent arrears recovery. All of the 15 local authorities participating in the research apply to the Benefits Agency to use direct payments as a method of recovering rent arrears from tenants on Income Support. Many reported that the proportion of tenants having direct payments had risen substantially over recent years. One council, for example, had experienced a five-fold increase, from 700 in 1991 to 3,500 in 1993. The increase in the number of tenants having direct payments was variously attributed by each council to higher rents; the growth in unemployment; and council policy to reduce the total level of rent arrears outstanding.

Council policies on the use of direct payments varied. Some councils offered tenants the opportunity of trying an alternative method prior to requesting direct payments whereas others sought direct payments from the outset.

To consider a direct payment for an individual tenant, a local authority must know that he or she is in receipt of Income Support. The vast majority of councils participating in the research relied first on tenants to inform the housing department that they were receiving Income Support. In addition, most authorities would arrange for a housing officer to visit a tenant's home prior to any enforcement proceedings where the tenant's benefit status was unknown. One council, however operated as an 'integrated benefits authority' and used Housing Benefit data to identify those tenants who were in receipt of Income Support.

A minority of local authorities opted to use direct payments only if an alternative payment arrangement failed. These councils who used direct payments as a last resort preferred to use weekly or fortnightly payment arrangements which were generally set at an equivalent level to direct payments. We also found that some councils were willing to accept less than the current direct payment rate where they thought it was in the best interest of the tenant. These councils tended to have anti-poverty strategies and have rent-recovery staff trained in debt counselling. Accepting lower payments towards clearing arrears from certain tenants was therefore part of council policy to reduce the level of poverty.

Administration of direct payments

Most of the councils reported good relationships with local Benefits Agency offices. Two councils had co-operated with local offices to design the forms used to assess whether people are entitled to direct payments. Many councils, however, reported that they had experienced specific problems with the service provided by the Benefits Agency. First, some councils reported that they were concerned about the length of time that they had to wait for the Benefits Agency to process applications for direct payments. During this time the arrears owed to the council could increase. Secondly, some staff thought that they received an inconsistent service from local Benefits Agency offices particularly in relation to the criteria used to accept or reject applications for direct payments. In the opinion of some staff it would be easier to negotiate with one regional agency rather than a number of district offices.

Many staff thought that non-dependant arrears should be liable for direct payments. Since direct payments are made only at £2.20, it is possible for some tenants to accrue arrears in excess of £18 per week while on direct payments. Clearly, the tenant will have to make their own arrangements to ensure that the non-dependant contribution is paid: otherwise they may still face eviction or distraint. In practice, the majority of local authorities participating in the research did not request direct payments for tenants with non-dependant arrears.

Several staff thought that arrears of former tenants should also be liable for direct payments. As Table 6.4 shows, arrears owed by former tenants accounts for over a third of all rent arrears outstanding to local authorities.

Many staff thought that recipients should be allowed to continue to use direct payments for fuel and water charges after they had finished paying off any arrears. Staff reported that in many cases recipients were put back on to direct payments within a few weeks of the Benefits Agency terminating direct payments. This results in additional administration for the local authority and the Benefits Agency.

Most staff believed that the current deduction of £2.20 was satisfactory, although some thought that the qualifying period and level of debt should be reduced so that arrears are 'nipped in the bud'. Currently arrears must amount to four times the weekly rent and have accumulated over at least eight weeks.

Finally, all of the staff interviewed reported that they would support extending the number of people who are eligible for direct payments. As direct payments were often viewed as the most cost-effective method of debt recovery, staff thought that extending the scheme to other low-income groups would save the local authority money. In particular it was felt that recipients of Invalidity Benefit should be allowed to use direct payments.

In summary, all the local authorities contacted for the study used direct payments to collect rent arrears, although some used the service as a last resort. While most reported good relationships with local Benefits Agency offices, many still reported problems with the service provided. In particular it was thought that problems were caused by the length of time taken to process claims and inconsistency between offices in payment methods. Many councils would like to see direct payments continue for tenants who have cleared outstanding arrears; a reduction in the qualifying period and the amount of arrears required; and coverage extended to non-dependant and former tenant arrears.

Community Charge arrears:

Number of direct payments

The number of recipients having direct payments for Community Charge arrears has grown from 58,000 in May 1991 to 243,000 in May 1992 (ASE, 1992).

Policies and attitudes towards direct payments for Community Charge arrears

Local authorities must apply for a liability order from a magistrates' court prior to seeking direct payments. Whereas all the local authorities contacted in the survey applied to the Benefits Agency for direct payments to recover Community Charge arrears from individuals receiving Income Support, some used direct payments only as a last resort. One local authority, for instance, used direct payments only if bailiffs could not recover sufficient goods to the value of the arrears outstanding. Other councils generally used direct payments prior to employing bailiffs. Most of the councils contacted in the survey used liability orders to make direct payments compulsory only if alternative payment methods failed. Those councils which used direct payments prior to employing bailiffs generally viewed direct payments as the most cost-effective method of debt recovery.

One treasury officer explained that in the absence of direct payments, once a liability order has been made, alternative debt-collection methods would not be cost-effective to the local authority. This is due to additional legal costs even though such costs are recoverable from the debtor.

> If it was taken away tomorrow (the direct payments service) it would mean that recovering money from people on Income Support would become uneconomical to the council, because every time we take legal action against someone there are legal costs involved and we have to add that to the debtors liability. Now if you're only recovering something like, say £60, your legal costs are fixed, they're not a percentage of the debt, so you can be adding another £60 on...it's costing you £60 to collect £60.

Although the Community Charge has now been replaced by the Council Tax, councils' estimates of how long it would take to clear all Community Charge arrears varied between five and eight years. Current legislation, however, only allows local authorities to initiate recovery of this money until 1998 (that is within six years of when the charge was due).

Administration of direct payments for Community Charge arrears

The local authorities contacted were generally satisfied with the level of service they received from the Benefits Agency and reported few problems. These mainly concerned delays by the Agency when responding to liability orders for direct payments, and the Agency's practice of making direct payments 13 weeks in arrears. Some councils would prefer to receive direct payments at more frequent intervals.

All of the staff interviewed thought that direct payments should be extended to other low-income groups receiving benefit. It was acknowledged that administration costs for

LIVERPOOL JOHN MOORES UNIVERSITY

the DSS would rise and that local authorities would probably be unwilling to pay for the services. Nevertheless it was generally thought that this would protect many more people from sanctions and reduce local authority debt recovery costs.

Some of the officials interviewed for the research thought that the administration of direct payments would be made easier if local authorities did not have to request a joint liability order from the court in cases where more than one partner was liable for Community Charge payments. Staff believed that direct payments could be made by one partner in these circumstances.

Although under the new Council Tax, Income Support claimants are entitled to a 100 per cent rebate, direct payments can still be used to recover Council Tax arrears accrued by the recipient prior to claiming Income Support.

Electricity companies

Number of direct payments

In May 1992, 95,000 recipients were having direct payments for electricity arrears and/or current consumption.

Number and size of arrears

Electricity companies do not produce statistics showing the number and level of arrears owing to them. Berthoud and Kempson (1992) in their national study of credit and debt, estimated that two per cent of domestic customers experienced a problem debt in 1988. Their survey showed that fuel debts were more strongly associated with poverty than any other household commitment. Electricity debts were also found to be closely related to the size of bills, with only one per cent of bills up to £5 per week causing repayment problems compared with over five per cent of bills of £10 and over.

Disconnections

The number of households disconnected for non-payment of electricity bills has fallen dramatically over recent years. In the year to March 1990, 80,000 households were disconnected, but in the year to March 1993 this figure had fallen to just over 12,000 (Figure 6.1).

Figure 6.1   Disconnection of domestic customers for each quarter (Great Britain)

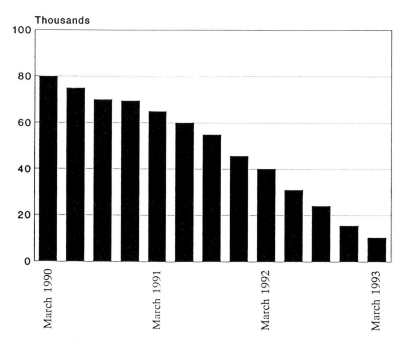

Source: OFFER, 1993

Disconnection levels vary by electricity company. During the year to March 1993 on average throughout Great Britain, 61 customers in every 10,000 were disconnected. However, this figure ranged from 27 in 10,000 for East Midlands to 187 in 10,000 for Northern Electricity (OFFER, 1993).

Policy and attitudes towards direct payments

Electricity companies vary widely in terms of their policies and attitudes towards direct payments. Our research shows that electricity companies essentially adopt one of two approaches. These we term the 'residual' and the 'option' approaches.

Electricity companies who adopt a 'residual' approach to direct payments generally prefer alternative methods of arrears collection, particularly pre-payment meters, and allow only those customers for whom alternative payment arrangements are impractical to use direct payments. Typically these companies restrict access to direct payments to those individuals who are disabled, have mobility problems, or find it difficult to access recharging and token outlets. Some companies reported that they might insist on a pre-payment meter for some disabled customers if another member of the household was able-bodied and could access recharging sites. Companies adopting this 'residual' approach are mainly based in the Midlands and South East England (Table 6.5).

Electricity companies who adopt an 'option'-based approach to direct payments are predominantly based in the North of England and Scotland (Table 6.5). These companies are less restrictive in terms of granting access to direct payments and generally allow Income Support recipients to opt to use them if requested. The explanation offered by electricity company staff as to why some adopt a 'residual' while others adopt an 'option' approach relates to historical precedent. Electricity companies in the North of England and Scotland (Hydro) have always had a high proportion of customers using direct payments compared with those in other regions. In addition some staff thought that pre-payment meters were not practical in some of the more rural areas of Scotland because customers would have to travel long distances to obtain tokens or recharge keys. The electricity companies that we contacted reported that they were unlikely to change their policy regarding direct payments in the near future.

Pre-payment meters were most likely to be used by Scottish Power and MANWEB, but least likely to be used by the Northern Electricity company. Weekly and fortnightly budget accounts were most likely to be used by Northern Electricity and least by Southern and SWEB. Over a third (36 per cent) of all electricity company customers used a payment scheme ranging from under a third in SEEB, Southern and MANWEB to over half (53 per cent) in Northern.

Administration of direct payments

All of the staff interviewed reported that they had very few problems associated with the administration of direct payments. Electricity company staff reported that they generally had a very good relationship with local Benefits Agency offices, although joint meetings have ceased in both areas 3 and 2 because too few customers were having direct payments.

Staff reported that one of the principal problems associated with direct payments is the additional arrears and administration associated with increased fuel consumption by people on direct payments. In these circumstances electricity company staff have to contact the customer and the Benefits Agency to arrange higher direct payments. If the Agency refuse to increase these payments the customer will be taken off direct payments and may be in a worse position than they were when they originally came on to the scheme.

Many staff thought that because of the availability of alternative payment methods, particularly pre-payment meters, any withdrawal of the direct payment scheme would have a relatively small impact on the level of arrears recovered from Income Support recipients. Some staff were concerned that people with learning difficulties could find it difficult to use pre-payment meters and thought that direct payments should be made an option for them.

Table 6.5 Percentage of domestic customers using payment schemes, March 1993

Scheme	London	SEEB	Southern	SWEB	S. Wales	MANWEB	Eastern	East Mids	MEB	NORWEB	Yorkshire	Northern	ScotP	Hydro	All
Direct payments	*	*	*	*	*	*	*	*	*	+	+	1	2	2	*
Meters	14	7	9	9	12	16	8	10	12	10	8	4	20	11	9
Monthly standing order, direct debit, cheque, cash	17	21	27	20	23	23	22	21	24	29	22	28	19	16	23
Weekly/fortnightly	1	2	+	+	7	1	*	3	2	5	4	11	1	4	1
Saving stamps	2	2	1	3	7	3	2	2	3	5	3	9	1	4	3
% of domestic customers	**34**	**32**	**37**	**32**	**49**	**43**	**32**	**36**	**41**	**49**	**38**	**53**	**43**	**45**	**36**

Source: OFFER (1993)
* <0.05
+ <0.5

Several staff personally thought that, although this was at odds with general company policy, direct payments should be made available to other low-income groups who were not in receipt of Income Support, and that recipients should be allowed to continue having direct payments when they had paid off the outstanding arrears.

In summary, electricity companies differ in their approach to the use of direct payments. Those companies who adopt an 'option' approach, consider direct payments to be an important element in arrears recovery, while those companies who adopt a 'residual' approach offer direct payments only to those Income Support recipients for whom a pre-payment meter is not deemed suitable. The electricity companies who adopt an 'option' approach reported that it was unlikely that they would change their policy regarding direct payments in the foreseeable future. All the electricity companies contacted reported that customers' increased consumption was the most serious problem with direct payments.

British Gas

Number of direct payments

In May 1992, 192,000 recipients were having direct payments for gas arrears and/or current consumption.

Number and size of arrears

British Gas do not produce statistics detailing the number and level of arrears owed to them. For information about arrears we therefore have to turn to other sources. Berthoud and Kempson (1992), on the basis of their survey, estimate that two per cent of domestic customers experienced problems paying for their gas in 1989. They also found that unlike electricity arrears, gas arrears were not particularly associated with the size of bills.

Gas disconnections

Gas disconnections have fallen dramatically over recent years. From a peak of 60,778 in 1987, they fell to 19,379 in 1989 and to 15,707 in 1992. Figure 6.2 shows the annual disconnection rate as a percentage of the overall domestic customers, and demonstrates that between 1988 and 1992 the level of disconnections fell from more than three customers in every thousand to under one customer in every thousand.

Figure 6.2   Annual disconnection rate as per cent of customer base

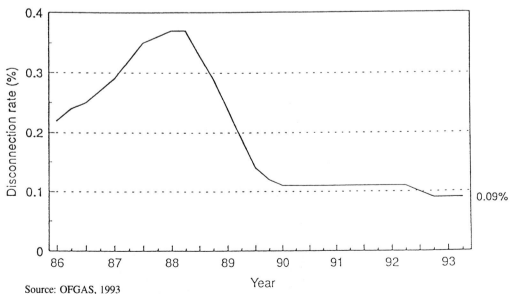

Source: OFGAS, 1993

Attitudes and policy regarding direct payments

British Gas view direct payments as a cost-effective method of recovering arrears from Income Support recipients. They publicise the scheme and send out information about direct payments to customers who are in arrears and all regional companies allow customers in receipt of Income Support to use direct payments.

The proportion of domestic customers having direct payments is very similar between British Gas regions (Table 6.6), between one and two per cent. On average five per cent used a pre-payment meter, this proportion however varies from three per cent in Scotland and Southern regions to seven per cent in Wales. Similarly the proportion paying by a payment plan ranged from less than a third in the North Eastern region to almost half in the Scottish region.

Table 6.6 Percentage of domestic gas customers using alternative payment methods by region, September 1993

Region	Fuel direct	Payment plan	Pre-payment meter	Other
	%	%	%	%
Scotland	2	49	3	44
Northern	2	44	5	49
North Western	2	37	6	55
North Eastern	2	32	4	62
East Midlands	1	34	5	60
West Midlands	1	34	4	61
Wales	2	33	7	58
Eastern	1	33	4	62
North Thames	1	29	6	64
South Eastern	1	45	5	49
Southern	1	46	3	50
South Western	1	36	4	59
All regions	**1**	**36**	**5**	**58**

Source: British Gas, 1993

Most staff reported that they preferred direct payment schemes to alternative methods of payment such as budget schemes because in their experience many people failed to keep to budget payments.

> *We'd rather they go on fuel direct as that way we know that way the money is guaranteed. With budget customers we don't always get the money in and often we then have to put them on direct payments anyway. (Team leader debt collection, area 3)*

Other staff thought that it was in the customer's best interests to try a budget payment plan prior to using direct payments.

Due to a variety of problems with pre-payment meters staff were also sceptical about using these as a method to recover arrears. Pre-payment meters for gas present specific technological problems different from electricity meters. In particular they are expensive to maintain and recover arrears as a proportion of current consumption, rather than at a set weekly rate. Many staff believed however that the 'Quantum' meter, which is currently being piloted in all British Gas regions, and which is more technologically advanced than conventional gas pre-payment meters, may provide a viable alternative to direct payments. Currently there are approximately 80,000 'Quantum' meters in operation.

Administration of direct payments

Staff were generally pleased with the level of service received from the Benefits Agency. In some regions regular joint meetings were held with Agency staff to discuss issues of mutual concern, and staff from British Gas headquarters regularly meet with DSS to discuss policy and practice.

Staff did however report a number of problems with administering the direct payment scheme. They thought that many people increased their consumption when using direct payments which could result in higher arrears. Many were concerned that the scheme was not explained clearly enough and that some Income Support recipients may be under the impression that all their consumption would be paid by the Benefits Agency. Staff thought the Benefits Agency should produce a publication outlining all the implications of fuel direct.

In one region staff reported that incorrect reference numbers attached to payment schedules caused additional administration. There was a belief that administrative mistakes and delays were caused by the under resourcing of Benefits Agency offices. In the same region it was reported that variations in local Benefits Agency office administrative procedures caused problems, in particular the timing of payments to British Gas and requests for estimates of customers' fuel consumption. Staff generally preferred the 'old system' where the Benefits Agency used a liaison officer to represent all the local offices.

Some staff felt aggrieved that the rules governing 'dual payments' had recently changed. The rules governing the operation of the schemes now permit only one direct payment for fuel. Previously British Gas could receive the equivalent of two direct payments from recipients who did not also have electricity payments. Some staff believed that if only one fuel direct payment was being paid the recipient would still have sufficient available income to pay the equivalent of two.

In summary, British Gas view direct payments as a cost-effective method of arrears recovery for Income Support recipients. Staff did however experience a number of problems with fuel direct, including recipients accruing higher arrears once on direct payments plus administrative delays and mistakes by the Benefits Agency over payments. In the future the development of more sophisticated pre-payment meters such as the 'Quantum' meter may make direct payments less desirable for British Gas.

Water companies

Number and size of direct payments

In May 1992, 132,000 recipients were having direct payments for water arrears and amenity charges, more than four times the number in May 1991.

Disconnections

Disconnections of domestic water supply have been increasing almost continuously since 1984 (the first time figures were published). Between 1984–85 and 1991–92 disconnections of domestic water supply increased more than ten-fold, from just over 2,000 to more than 21,000. Over the last year however there has been a slight fall (Table 6.7).

Table 6.7   Household disconnections for non-payment of water rates/charges

	Number
1984–85	2,052
1985–86	4,212
1986–87	6,450
1987–88	7,120
1988–89	8,270
1989–90	10,013
1990–91	7,673
1991–92	21,286
1992–93	18,636

Source: OFWAT, 1993

Policies and attitudes towards direct payments

Staff from all of the water companies reported that they viewed direct payments as an important method of recovering arrears from customers receiving Income Support. For four of the companies contacted the number of customers having direct payments had increased substantially over the last year. The increases were attributed to a variety of causes including the company publicising the availability of direct payments; increased water charges; and the removal of water charges from local authority rents.

Companies did not openly publicise the availability of direct payments except for those customers in serious arrears who were informed about their availability prior to disconnection. Whereas some companies preferred recipients to use direct payments if they were in arrears, others used direct payments as a last option and only when recipients had failed to keep to an instalment plan. Because of their limited availability, pre-payment meters were not considered a viable alternative to direct payments. However some staff believed that if the number of pre-payment meters increased then they could become an acceptable alternative.

Administration of direct payments

Staff from water companies reported that they were generally satisfied with the level of service provided by the Benefits Agency. All of the companies contacted had regular joint meetings to discuss areas of mutual concern. Staff did, however, believe that the direct payment service could be improved in certain ways. First all staff were concerned at the priority ordering of direct payments. Currently direct payments for water cannot be paid if the recipient has housing, gas and electricity direct payments. Staff thought that water was an essential service and should have the same priority as housing and fuel.

> We don't see water as being any different from gas or electricity, we don't see that water is any less a priority, in fact we could perhaps argue that it's more of a priority than gas and electricity. (Accounts supervisor, area 2).

Although the problem was not widespread (fewer than one per cent of applicants are refused on grounds of low priority), it was reported that a few Income Support recipients had been disconnected because they had been refused direct payments by the Benefits Agency.

Two companies reported that they had experienced long delays in receiving decisions on applications for direct payments, and in getting money transferred from the Benefits Agency.

All of the staff interviewed supported the extension of direct payments to low-income customers who were not currently in receipt of Income Support, as they thought this would prevent the possibility of disconnection and guarantee payments. None of the staff interviewed thought that the water company would be willing to pay for an extension to the service.

Summary and policy options

Third-party creditors have differing attitudes and policies towards the use of direct payments. Indeed within the same service sector local company policy can vary widely. Similarly the range of problems associated with direct payments can also differ between companies. All of the creditors discussed in this chapter, with the possible exception of certain regional electricity companies, viewed direct payments as an essential part of debt recovery. The majority of creditors participating in the survey also reported that the number of customers using direct payments had increased substantially.

The relative cost-effectiveness of alternative payment options necessarily determines the degree to which creditors support direct payments. In the experience of many, weekly or fortnightly budget schemes are in many cases not adhered to by customers receiving Income Support and this is also borne out by the experiences of people discussed in Chapter Five. With the exception of electricity companies, direct payments are viewed as the most cost-effective method of debt recovery and are often preferred to budget schemes. Electricity companies by contrast view pre-payment meters as more cost-effective than direct payments since they prevent the possibility of increased arrears and are economical to maintain. These financial savings to electricity companies, however, are not passed on to customers who pay a higher standing charge and incur the added costs associated with obtaining tokens and recharging keys. Technological advances in the design of pre-payment meters for water and gas may result in reducing the reliance that these sectors currently have on direct payments as a method of debt recovery.

Apart from mortgage lenders who currently pay for the service, we found that in the personal opinion of most staff, third-party creditors would be unlikely to pay for the direct payment schemes, even though many acknowledged that they serve as a debt-collection service. Other staff did not know how their organisation would react in response to a charge levied on the service. No one interviewed thought that their organisation definitely would pay for direct payments.

Although creditors are generally satisfied with the quality of service provided by the Benefits Agency, our research has revealed a range of problems that are common to all or most third parties. These are grouped into themes and discussed below.

Access

Problems related to Income Support recipients gaining access to direct payments were reported by most creditors. When people are refused access to direct payments local authorities and the utilities must make alternative methods of payment available, many of which are not thought to be as cost-effective. Some third-party creditors thought that the Benefits Agency stipulated too high an arrears figure and too long a qualifying period for direct payments to be made. Several also thought that direct payments should be made available to recipients prior to getting into arrears and that those already on direct payments should be able to choose to continue with them after arrears had been cleared.

Creditors generally supported the extension of direct payments to other low-income recipients currently excluded from direct payments. As we show in Chapter Seven this view is also held by some Benefits Agency staff. In addition, local authorities would also like to see non-dependant arrears and former tenant arrears subject to direct payments.

Administrative errors and delays

All of the third party creditors reported that they incurred additional administrative costs because of mistakes by the Benefits Agency. These usually related to incorrect identification numbers, but sometimes included non-payment or under- and over-payments. There was a general feeling among third parties that these mistakes were due to the Benefits Agency under-resourcing direct payment sections. (Conversely, administrative mistakes by third parties also cause additional work for Benefits Agency staff as we will discuss in Chapter Seven.) In addition many third parties complained of the length of time taken by the Benefits Agency to process applications and notify them of the outcome.

Possible policy options to reduce these problems include ensuring that minimum response times are met and introducing service level agreements between third parties and the Benefits Agency so that both receive and can depend upon a high quality service.

Consistency of service

Many creditors complained of variations in the policy toward direct payment administration of local Benefits Agency offices and the level of service provided by them. These problems were particularly acute for creditors who deal with many local offices. Problems are caused because local offices adopt different administrative arrangements concerning the timing of payments. Creditors would prefer all payments from local offices to arrive on the same day so that the time devoted to processing direct payments could be minimised.

Creditors also complained about variations in decisions by adjudication officers concerning access to schemes. Some local offices were thought to adopt more stringent eligibility criteria than others. This sometimes caused resentment between creditor staff and Benefits Agency staff. Some variation in decision making is not surprising since adjudication officers must interpret and make judgements about some difficult areas of law. However, there is possibly a case for the Chief Adjudication Officer to monitor direct payment decisions more closely, perhaps in a special exercise. In addition the Benefits Agency could ensure that all third parties are fully informed of the rules governing eligibility for the schemes.

Another option to reduce these problems is to set up a regional contact point so that each creditor could discuss local administration and decision making with Benefits Agency staff. This may help to provide a more standardised service for creditors.

There is also scope for creditors to change their organisational practices so that they are more effective in dealing with local Benefits Agency offices.

Priority ordering

Water companies reported that they were not satisfied with the current priority ordering of direct payments. They argue that because water is an essential service it should be given as high a priority ordering as fuel.

One option available to the Benefits Agency is to re-order the priority by which direct payments are made, so that water has equal status to that of fuel. To promote consumer choice the responsibility for deciding the relative priority between fuel and water direct payments could be given to the consumer. Alternatively a *pro rata* system could be introduced on a similar basis to the one used by money advisers to distribute available income to creditors. Recipients could be assessed as having a certain level of available income and this could be shared out to third parties in relation to the outstanding arrears. Such a policy would have the benefit of protecting Income Support recipients from all third-party sanctions, but it would create a large increase in administration if payments needed to be rescheduled frequently.

In this chapter we have considered the views and practices of third-party creditors regarding direct payments and outlined a number of policy options which might benefit them. The following chapter considers the Benefits Agency perspective. In Chapter Eight we attempt to draw together the views of all parties (including creditors, Benefits Agency staff and recipients) in evaluating the policy options for the future of direct payments.

Chapter 7   Benefits Agency Perspectives

Introduction

In this chapter we discuss the experiences, perceptions, and opinions of Benefits Agency staff who are routinely involved with the day-to-day administration of direct payments. It draws upon qualitative information derived from interviews with staff from three local Benefits Agency offices. In these interviews we explored five issues relevant to policy and planning in this area:

- How do staff administer the various schemes, and what problems do they encounter when processing direct payments?

- When administering direct payments, what contact do staff have with Income Support recipients?

- What sort of relationship do staff have with third-party creditors?

- What are the views of staff concerning the positive and negative aspects of direct payments?

- Do staff think the direct payments service could be improved?

We discuss each of these issues in turn and draw together the main policy issues concerning the administration of direct payments arising from our research. Prior to outlining the findings from our interviews we present a profile of the direct payments caseloads of the three offices used in the study.

The size of caseload varied widely between the three offices, with the office in area 1 having a caseload three times that in area 3 and almost a third larger than the office in area 2 (Table 7.1). The relative proportion of direct payments between offices also varied. Community Charge arrears represented the largest proportion of the direct payment caseload in areas 1 and 2, compared with fuel in area 3. For all three offices, payments for rent arrears accounted for approximately a quarter of the caseload.

Table 7.1   Direct payment caseloads of three offices, April 1993

	Area 1		Area 2		Area 3	
	N	**%**	**N**	**%**	**N**	**%**
Gas	722	26	369	29	381	43
Electricity	72	3	26	2		
Water	387	14	97	5	82	9
Rent	666	24	472	23	223	25
Community Charge	930	33	814	41	132	17
Residential nursing home	0	0	0	0	55	6
Other	3	0	1	0	0	0
Total	**2,780**	**100**	**1,979**	**100**	**873**	**100**

Source: Benefits Agency local office statistics

Staff in all three offices reported that their direct payment caseloads had increased substantially over the previous year. In particular, direct payments for Community Charge arrears and rent arrears had shown a sharp increase. In area 1 for example the caseload had more than doubled over the last 12 months, with a seven-fold increase in payments for Community Charge arrears and a 200 per cent increase for rent arrears. Staff reported that their work had become more complex and demanding. This was attributed to the recent changes in the number and range of direct payments.

How decisions are made

Although direct payment schemes are governed by prescribed rules and regulations, adjudication officers are still required to exercise an element of discretion or judgement in their decisions. In Chapter Three we discussed the decision-making processes used by staff when deciding to accept or reject applications for direct payments. In this chapter we focus on the decision-making criteria used by staff to determine whether direct payments should continue for people who have repaid arrears.

The decision to continue direct payments

Normally, direct payments are discontinued for Income Support recipients who have repaid arrears, although some continue at the discretion of the adjudication officer. In our interviews we attempted to identify the criteria used by staff to determine whether direct payments continue or stop.

For the most part staff thought it was generally in someone's best interests to resume responsibility for current liability once arrears have been cleared. Staff also reported however that they would usually continue direct payments for specific groups of 'vulnerable' people. These included physically disabled people, people with learning difficulties and those who were thought to be incapable of budgeting for themselves.

Staff reported that they usually based their decisions on whether to reject applications or continue direct payments on information already contained in their own records, for example, if a disability premium was paid as part of Income Support. Information was also occasionally provided by social workers and probation officers, but staff reported that they did not actively seek information from outside agencies.

Several staff thought that the principal reason for discontinuing direct payments for the majority of recipients was to reduce the administrative workload. The supervisor in area 3 explained this position:

> *The main reason I would look to be tending to take them off...the criteria that I use for that is we'd need an army in here to maintain all these direct payments, if we kept everyone adding on...We've got to clear some people and give someone else a chance.*

Other staff reported that in their experience it was often more cost-effective to continue direct payments for some people, because it was likely that many of them would soon accrue arrears and re-apply. Since setting up a direct payment is the most time-consuming aspect of their administration, a cycle of stopping and starting a payment was considered inefficient.

It seems, therefore, that current policy concerning the continuation of direct payments is necessarily a compromise between the control of administrative costs and promoting financial independence on the one hand, and providing customer choice and budgeting assistance on the other. Evidence from our interviews suggests that continuing direct payments for more Income Support recipients would promote customer choice. The effect on administrative costs is harder to judge since any savings from not having to re-instate people with further arrears would be offset by the cost of maintaining payments for those whose arrears have been cleared.

Contact with claimants

When administering direct payments, staff routinely contact Income Support recipients to provide and elicit information. This contact is principally by standard letters, sent to people when setting up direct payments or when notifying them of any changes in the level of deductions. The Benefits Agency do not keep people informed about the level of arrears outstanding. It is the responsibility of third parties to provide this information.

Also, people on direct payments frequently contact the Benefits Agency concerning a variety of problems. Contact is usually by telephone, but people also send letters and visit the office in person. Staff reported that the majority of problems were about the initial stages of setting up direct payments, and that relatively few people contacted them with problems once direct payments were in operation.

> *We're always getting people 'phoning up who've got problems. But it's not so much people once they're on, they know what they want, the paperwork that's given should be sufficient in most circumstances for them to understand. And as long as the bills come in and show credit paid by DSS they're quite happy. (Adjudication officer, area 2)*

> *We do get some queries, you get the odd one who wants to know how much you've sent to them, but really once it's running smoothly, it's very few queries really. (Adjudication officer, area 3)*

Many people contacting the Benefits Agency were concerned to prevent disconnection or eviction. Often, an approach for assistance was only made immediately prior to the enforcement of creditor sanctions. When this occurred staff were put under pressure to act quickly and prevent disconnection or eviction taking place.

> *They do ring up, they just say 'I'm in arrears, can you help me?'. I mean a lot of them leave it to the very last minute, some of them even wait, would you believe it, 'til they've actually been disconnected before they approach us. (Adjudication officer, area 2)*

> *I think they usually 'phone in desperation, they're going to be cut off and this is the only way that they can stop being cut off. (Adjudication officer, area 3)*

For the most part, staff thought that the information provided for people on direct payments was usually sufficient for them to understand what was happening. Once a payment had been set up contact was usually made to enquire about current arrears or to question recent changes in the level of payments. Occasionally people contacted the Benefits Agency because they had been notified by a third party that direct payments had not been made.

The supervisor from area 1 explained that, on the whole, people do understand direct payment schemes, and for those who did not, a short explanation was usually sufficient to solve any problems.

> *They do understand the schemes...but those who don't, a quick explanation and they've got it straight away. I mean it's quite simple. We deduct a certain amount from your benefit and pay that direct to the third party. Your order book as a result will be reduced by ten pounds and they're quite happy with an explanation like that.*

In summary, people contacted the Benefits Agency over specific problems associated with direct payments. Contact was largely confined to the initial processing of applications and most staff believed that the level of information provided to recipients was satisfactory.

The relationship between the Benefits Agency and third parties

Third-party creditors are at liberty to withdraw from direct payment schemes if they are not satisfied with the service provided by the Benefits Agency. However, additional administration could be reduced for both parties if each are made aware of the other's policies and practices regarding direct payments. In the following section we discuss the relationship between the Benefits Agency and each of the principal third parties who are paid direct.

Local Authorities

Local authorities can receive direct payments for arrears of rent, Community Charge and Council Tax. Direct payments for Community Charge and Council Tax arrears are usually administered by the treasury department and for rent arrears by the housing department. Although the Community Charge has now been replaced by the Council Tax, direct payments for arrears can continue to be made but the local authority will need to obtain the necessary liability order by 1998.

Rent arrears

The Benefits Agency offices in our study had good working relationships with local authorities. Staff from area 2 and area 3 reported that they occasionally had joint meetings with the local council to 'iron out any problems'. In area 1 the local council had contracted out their housing stock to local housing associations and staff reported that they had few problems and little contact with them.

However, Benefits Agency staff reported that problems did occasionally arise. In area 1, staff believed that the main problems centred around the local authority requesting direct payments for tenants with insufficient arrears to be eligible. This caused unnecessary work for the Benefits Agency as staff had to notify local authorities about each rejected application.

In area 2 staff had co-operated with the council to design a form that could be used by recipients when applying to use direct payments, and it was thought that this had made administration easier. The supervisor of the direct payments section explained its advantages:

> The relationship couldn't be improved really. We had a chat with them and they developed this request form, where they go out and see the person who's in arrears and the person signs up and agrees to a direct payment...We get a lot of rents now where they've signed up already agreeing to it . So we put it through, plus if there's more than four times the weekly rent in arrears, we automatically do it. And if there's court action to take away the tenancy, we can automatically do it because we've got to be looking at the claimant's interest. They've got to have somewhere to live, they may as well stop where they are, it's cheaper to everybody.

It may be of value to the Benefits Agency to monitor and publicise local initiatives such as this so that local offices in other areas may benefit.

Community Charge arrears

Direct payments for Community Charge arrears were the largest single direct payment in area 1 and area 2 and arrears had increased substantially in all three offices over recent years. Despite this increase, staff reported that they had very little contact with local authorities concerning the Community Charge. The supervisor in area 1 explained that the relationship with his local authority was a simple one and did not require close liaison.

> Poll tax arrears – we don't have a relationship with them as such, there's been no real need to have a contact point...because it's just really a case as per law, they bang us through all these liability orders and we, if we can take the deduction, we take it and it's as simple as that.

Staff identified few problems with the administration of direct payments for Community Charge arrears. However, some additional administration was caused through the practice of stopping direct payments only to start them again within a few months. In area 1 the local council had changed its policy on direct payments and was combining arrears for more than one year. The supervisor in area 1 explained how this policy reduced their workload.

> What we're finding we're doing is, we're clearing these arrears, we're taking them off and then within about a month a new liability order is coming through...What they seem to be doing now, the council is combining two years together, instead of doing one year at a time, which is far better for us because it stops us putting them on, taking them off, putting them on, taking them off.

Mortgage lenders

The Benefits Agency office in area 3 was alone in having a dedicated section to process direct payments for mortgage interest. In the other two offices direct payments were processed by the Income Support section.

The local offices did not have any joint meetings with local mortgage lenders and communication between lenders and the Benefits Agency was usually undertaken on an individual case basis, either by letter or over the telephone.

Benefits Agency staff highlighted a number of problems associated with the administration of direct payments for mortgage lenders. First, some staff admitted that due to administrative errors when processing information for the BACS system, lenders were frequently paid incorrect amounts. When this occurred, lenders usually contacted the mortgage holder to demand the missed payment and this often resulted in complaints to the Benefits Agency. Staff thought that it would be better for lenders to contact them first if there were any problems over payment.

Secondly, problems arose because some claimants (although required to do so) did not notify the Benefits Agency about changes in the interest rate. Recently, interest rates have been falling and this has resulted in overpayments to lenders and additional administration for the Benefits Agency when mistakes are eventually discovered and rectified.

In the experience of some staff, building societies were much more co-operative than banks when asked to provide information about customers.

> *If you want any information from a bank it's like getting blood out of a stone, they're not as co-operative as they could be...and you get problems getting information off the banks even if they are going to get paid off you...If I try to contact them by phone to get information I usually end up putting the phone down really frustrated because they want things in writing...Whereas a building society will give you the information and then follow it through with a letter, but they will give you the information.*

Staff reported that when direct payments for mortgage interest became generally automatic, they received many complaints from Income Support recipients, largely about loss of financial flexibility, though the number of these was now small.

Electricity companies

In the experience of staff from the three offices, electricity companies preferred to use alternative payment methods to direct payments. As a result the number of direct payments was relatively small, and most contact with electricity companies was on a case-by-case basis, usually by letter but sometimes by telephone. Joint meetings were reported to be rare, with only the local office in area 1 having recently arranged a meeting with electricity company staff.

Staff reported few problems in administering direct payments for electricity arrears, but said that it was often very difficult to get electricity companies to accept direct payments. The practice of restricting access to direct payments provoked a mixed response from staff. Some welcomed it because their workload was kept low.

> *We had a meeting with the electricity board pre-Christmas...to cut a long story short, what they were trying to say to us is 'We do not like direct payments, we prefer to collect our own debts'...And in a nutshell that's fine by us. We can concentrate on other areas if we don't have to bother with the electricity board. (Supervisor, area 1)*

Other staff thought that the electricity boards were very inflexible about access to direct payments and it was thought that for some Income Support recipients and their families, because of the possibility of self-disconnection, pre-payment meters were not always in their best interests.

British Gas

Staff in the three offices thought that they had a good working relationship with British Gas who, they felt, were keen to promote direct payments as a method of debt collection. This perceived enthusiasm caused resentment from some staff however.

> *The instant anyone gives them a bit of grief about 'I can't pay my bill,' question one is 'Are you on Income Support?' If the answer is yes – 'Go and see your social*

security office'. And it's as simple as that, and the figures will show we've got seven hundred on gas and seventy on electric. (Supervisor, area 1)

Staff reported that they frequently attended meetings with staff from British Gas to discuss areas of mutual concern. Some thought that the administration of direct payments could be improved if British Gas adopted a 'one stop' policy in relation to direct payments.

You've got the direct payments section that we normally deal with, we get on quite well with those. But then when you've got ancillaries that you don't deal with very often and it doesn't appear that anyone from the direct payment section will say 'Well you normally deal with me'...it's not one stop shall we say, as we talk about here in our department, where you say 'Leave it with me and I'll get it sorted out'. (Supervisor, area 2)

Staff reported that, occasionally, they did get complaints from Income Support recipients or money advice agencies about British Gas overestimating current consumption. On the whole staff endeavoured to contact British Gas to resolve the problem. However, they have no means of checking estimates and no authority to insist on lower direct payments for current consumption. Gas customers who continued to be dissatisfied with the situation were referred to OFGAS.

Water companies

Staff in the three Benefits Agency offices reported that they generally had good relationships with local water companies. In their experience, water companies were increasingly using direct payments as a method of reducing arrears figures.

Staff from two of the local offices had recently attended meetings with local water companies to discuss administrative arrangements for direct payments. The supervisor in area 1 found these meetings helpful because it gave him an opportunity to plan his future workload.

And what we were doing, the reason we were meeting with them was it was a forewarning for us that 'Look you're going get a lot of requests for water rates shortly because we're going be after these people'...Well thanks for the warning, that's number one, because sometimes we don't get warning about anything and we get an influx of stuff in and you've got three staff and you're snookered. So you've got to reorganise your work to take on this workload. But to be given the warning it gives us a chance.

Some staff reported that budget accounts were a viable alternative to direct payments and that they did not always implement requests from water boards if the recipient did not agree to it. For example, the Benefits Agency in area 1 send out a standard form (A75) asking, as a 'courtesy measure', whether the recipient wants help paying their water charges.

If someone says I don't want to go on to direct payments that's fine by me, as an adjudication officer I would go along with that and I'm all for people sorting themselves out if that's how they feel...He knows his best interests better than I do. (Supervisor, area 1)

Staff in the three areas did not consider pre-payment meters for water a viable option as they were not readily available.

In summary, the Benefits Agency offices in these three areas seemed to have a good working relationship with third-party creditors. Joint meetings were sometimes organised and staff were often on first-name terms with company staff. The practices of creditors did sometimes cause additional administrative problems for staff and there may be scope for these to be reduced by publicising successful local initiatives.

Staff views on the positive and negative aspects of direct payments

Through the course of their work Benefits Agency staff have first-hand experience of how direct payments are helpful or cause problems for Income Support recipients.

Staff believed that direct payments were useful for two main reasons; preventing creditor sanctions, and helping people to budget on low incomes. As the supervisor in area 2 explained:

I think that if you're on a small, tight fixed income that the benefits of having a fixed payment each week to meet your debts would probably far outweigh any other method of paying for it. Even on a weekly basis because bills don't come on a regular flow. In the winter, you take heating, it's far higher than it is in the summer. So it does to some extent help people to budget.

In the experience of staff, direct payments also had a number of negative aspects. Some staff supported the current policy to assist Income Support recipients at the point of crisis and return them to financial autonomy once arrears have been cleared. In their opinion, continuing payments or extending the schemes to other benefit recipients would encourage more people to become dependent on the social security system for their budgeting by taking away their choice and control of their personal finances.

I think a person is better off managing their own affairs. I think it's turning everyone into robots if everything was done for them...They have little to do when they don't have a job don't they, so therefore if they haven't even got to think about paying the bills or anything, it's taking their minds away in my opinion. (Supervisor, area 3)

We can intervene and assist them to get out of the muddle basically and get them back to zero again, and it's just like a helping hand basically. But what we try to do, is once we've given them that helping hand, is try and put them back where they're responsible for their own bills and they look after their own finances, which basically is what life's all about. If we took it over for all of them and all the utilities, then they'd become very welfare sort of minded wouldn't they, very state reliant and think that we do everything for you. (Supervisor, area 1)

Other staff thought that because of the inability of some people to manage their own financial affairs, current policy of stopping direct payments once arrears are repaid was a pointless exercise because many people would soon get in to financial difficulties and reapply.

The majority of people if they're already in that situation, they can't budget very well anyway. So us doing that would help them for the time they're on direct payments, but as soon as they're in credit again, they're going to get in a similar situation again...Nine times out of ten they'll be back on direct payments within three or four months. (Adjudication officer, area 1)

All staff agreed that Income Support recipients would experience budgeting difficulties in the absence of direct payments. Some staff thought that the level of benefit made it extremely difficult for people to budget, particularly those who were previously used to living on a much higher income. Direct payments in these circumstances help to ease the transition from employment to living on benefit.

In general people just get dropped in it. I mean if you're made redundant and you've been used to earning quite a lot of money...Say you've been working at the firm twelve months or less, once you've had your initial pay in lieu and then all of a sudden you're on a very small rate, and that can be a hell of a job to adjust to try and live on that money, and it's really, you know, I can see it being very difficult for these people. (Supervisor, area 1)

Other staff thought that low income levels caused financial difficulties for some Income Support recipients, who therefore needed direct payments if they wanted to retain essential services.

I don't think that these people are not capable of budgeting, I just don't think they've got enough money to budget. Well ideally they ought to have more money to budget themselves...And when it comes to it, they've got no choice about whether to go on to direct payments, because I mean if you've got three kids and they need food and clothes, then it's the electricity and gas that don't get paid. (Adjudication officer, area 3)

In summary, all staff thought that direct payments were useful to Income Support recipients because they helped prevent sanctions and aided budgeting. Several staff were concerned, however, that as a result of using direct payments, some people would become dependent on the social security system for budgeting. In addition some staff thought that low income levels left some people with little choice but to use direct payments.

Improvements and changes to the service

Staff in each of the three offices suggested possible improvements to the current administration of direct payments and changes to the structure of schemes. These included computer integration, the extension of direct payments to recipients of other social security benefits such as Invalidity Benefit, charging creditors for the service, and rescheduling the priority ordering.

Computer integration

Staff thought that many of the administrative problems associated with the processing of direct payments stemmed from a lack of integration between the computer system containing information about Income Support recipients and the system that administered payments to third-party creditors. In particular, transferring data between the two systems often resulted in incorrect amounts paid to creditors. An adjudication officer from area 3 explained how the two computer systems caused problems for her.

> *Most of our problems now are dealing with these two computers...The deductions are made on this computer, on this system...But the payments are made on that computer so we have a lot of cases where there's discrepancies between the two amounts. So you might be deducting £5 here and only £4.50 there...I mean they often twig the fact that they say 'I've been deducted £5.00 a week and the gas board say we're only paying them £4.00,' – we get an awful lot of that.*

The Benefits Agency have addressed this problem and have installed integrated computer processing of direct payments. These integrated systems should provide a higher quality of service to all parties by reducing the number of errors associated with the manual transfer of data between systems.

Extending direct payments

Some staff thought that direct payment schemes should be extended to other low-income benefit recipients, in particular those receiving Invalidity Benefit. There was a feeling amongst some staff that direct payments could help anyone with a low income. Supervisors reported, however, that they would need extra staff to undertake the additional workload.

> *There's a helping hand for the ones just below (Income Support) and suddenly that helping hand is taken away isn't it. For the ones just above it seems very unfair. But again I look at the point of view from the technical point of view, if you do this for all benefits, I think you need an army of people to actually maintain these deductions. (Supervisor, area 1)*

Other staff thought that direct payments should only be extended to other groups if the creditor companies were required to pay for the service.

Charging third-party creditors

Staff were in general agreement that creditors should be charged for the direct payments service. Most staff viewed their work as a form of debt collection for third parties. Several staff thought that revenue generated from charging could be used to support and expand the direct payments service provided by the Benefits Agency. At present only mortgage lenders contribute towards the cost of direct payments.

Priority ordering

Staff generally thought that the current priority ordering of direct payments served people's best interests. Some believed however that water direct payments should be ranked as high as those for fuel. Currently water payments cannot be paid if there are already three direct payments for housing and fuel debts, and this leaves some recipients vulnerable to disconnection. Staff reported that this was not a common problem at present but many thought that it could be in the near future as charges rise and as water companies become increasingly diligent in their pursuit of debtors.

Summary

The recent growth in the number and range of direct payments has increased the pressures and demands placed upon staff who must strive to provide a high-quality service while managing more complex workloads.

Income Support recipients experience problems with direct payments and contact the Benefits Agency. These problems are largely confined to the initial stages of setting up direct payments and few problems are reported once direct payments are operating.

Many of the problems associated with the processing of direct payments, particularly incorrect payments, are attributed to mistakes when transferring data between computer systems. These problems are being addressed by the installation of integrated computer systems for the administration of direct payments.

Whereas most staff thought that it was generally in a recipient's best interests to resume responsibility for current liability once arrears had been cleared, several staff thought that it would be more cost-effective to continue direct payments for some people.

The three offices generally had good working relationships with local third-party creditors and sometimes arranged meetings to discuss areas of mutual concern. Problems did arise however when creditors, particularly electricity companies, refused to accept direct payments for individuals on Income Support. We identified a number of local initiatives to overcome such problems. The Benefits Agency may find it useful to monitor and publicise innovatory local initiatives between district offices and creditors so that other areas may benefit from good practice.

Through the course of their work, Benefits Agency staff have first-hand experience of how direct payments are beneficial to Income Support recipients and creditors. In the light of this, staff identified a number of possible changes to the present direct payments system. These include extending direct payments to other benefit recipients, charging some creditors for the service and changing the current priority ordering of direct payments. These possibilities are discussed further in Chapter Eight.

Chapter 8   Policy Options

Direct payments from benefit for fuel and rent arrears were originally designed as last resort measures to prevent disconnection from fuel supplies or homelessness, and it is clear that the current policy of the DSS still sees them in this light. However, since the original fuel and rent direct schemes were introduced there has been a substantial change in the range and scope of deductions from benefit. Direct payments are now possible for water charges, Community Charge and Council Tax arrears, child maintenance, unpaid fines and mortgage interest payments. Only payments for water charges fall into the same category as fuel and rent direct, as a last resort payment to prevent disconnection. Payments for Community Charge arrears and unpaid fines by deductions from benefit also serve a preventive function by removing the severe sanction of imprisonment. They are also consistent with the ruling that Community Charge arrears and unpaid fines can be recovered from earnings. Mortgage interest direct is comparable to Housing Benefit, being a transfer payment rather than a deduction from benefit, although it is still administered by the direct payment section.

The number of other deductions from benefit has also increased since the early days of fuel direct. The DSS has always recovered overpayments of benefit by deduction from current payments, but the replacement of single payments with Social Fund loans has considerably extended the use of deductions. Although the scope of this research does not extend beyond direct payments, these deductions are nevertheless relevant in considering the total effect of direct payments and deductions for people on Income Support, and also for the administration of the schemes.

Changes outside the social security system, but relevant to direct payments, have also occurred. The gas, electricity and water industries have been privatised. Although the aim of direct payments has never been debt collection they do operate to some extent in that way. When the utilities were state enterprises, there was some rationale in saving the state money by reducing the debt to nationalised industries. However, it is not the concern of the DSS to help private companies with their debt collection. Thus the sole justification for the schemes is still that they are of value to the people on Income Support.

Technical changes have also taken place. Pre-payment meters for electricity are more sophisticated and rechargeable card and token meters have largely overcome the problems of meter theft. This has led to a considerable decline in the number of direct payments for electricity. Electricity companies prefer that the electricity which is used is paid for and arrears do not mount up. Metering technology is not so far advanced for gas and water payment, but time will no doubt see the introduction of satisfactory meters here also.

Over a similar period, since the early 1980s, there has been general increase in indebtedness and a more widespread acceptance of debt (or credit) as a way of dealing with financial transactions. This may well be an additional factor in the other main change which has occurred – the overall rise in the numbers of deductions from benefit. The increase in the types of deductions and in the numbers of people in receipt of Income Support are probably the main reasons for this growth. However, the outcome is that more people have less money for their day-to-day expenditure and the administrative task of dealing with these deductions has increased substantially.

These changes to the context of the direct payment schemes raise questions about whether the schemes should change in response, and if so, how they could change.

There is a history in social security of arrangements which are originally intended to be the exception or last resort, expanding over time to involve more and more claimants, and absorbing considerable administrative time. Examples include exceptional circumstances allowances, single payments and the additional requirements for heating, and diet and so on. Income Support was designed to simplify all these arrangements. In this chapter we examine the possible options for direct payments in the light of these changes and the context of Income Support.

Policies with varying degrees of impact

The first policy question to ask, perhaps, is whether direct payments should continue or should they be abolished? There is a range of choices between these options, however, from relatively minor administrative changes to the existing system to more structural options involving changing the system in some way. For example, if the choice were to continue with direct payments, should they remain as they are or are there administrative changes which could be made to improve them. Whether the schemes should expand or contract is a more structural option. The option to abolish the schemes is an extreme of these choices. We will discuss the policy options for the direct payment schemes from the least change option to those involving more structural changes. The options are considered in the context of DSS concerns to promote independence and choice, to pursue value for money and to improve administrative efficiency and flexibility (DSS, 1993). Under the heading of administrative changes we will discuss continuing the schemes, leaving them unchanged and possibilities for their improvement. The options of reducing the schemes, abolishing them and expanding them are considered under the heading of structural changes. Running through all these policy options is a tension between imposition and choice, and policies which promote either one of these can be part of any of the contrasting choices outlined above. The final section discusses where opportunities for choice can be expanded.

Administrative changes

The first choice in deciding policy on the system of direct payments is whether it should continue or not; then, if it is to continue, should it be left alone or are there some administrative changes which would improve it?

Continuation

One of the key indicators in evaluating a service is whether those for whom it is intended, in this case those who use direct payments, find it useful or not. The respondents in our national survey of recipients of Income Support who have had experience of direct payments found them valuable in doing what they were designed to do – provide protection from creditor sanctions. Creditors interviewed also said that direct payments were an effective and reliable method of debt collection. Money advisers were perhaps less enthusiastic but felt that direct payments did help people on Income Support who were in debt and that hence they should continue. Thus at this very general level there was a great deal of support for the system of direct payments from benefit. Conversely no one interviewed said direct payments were a thoroughly bad idea and should be abolished immediately. Thus a necessary condition for the continuation of the schemes has been fulfilled – their usefulness to the claimant. This in itself provides a strong argument for their continuation. However, the decision to continue will also be based on the costs of running the schemes and their compatibility with wider government policies, such as increasing personal responsibility.

Leave alone

The first question to ask is how serious are the problems the research has revealed? To some extent the response of people who use direct payments suggests that the problems are not so serious as to outweigh the value of the schemes. However, there are difficulties in ensuring that correct payments are made in time, and that all three parties involved are clear about what payments are made. Other problems exist in the estimation of current consumption for fuel, the priority of payments, and lack of knowledge about the schemes. In the main the problems stem from the fact that the operation of direct payments is complex, involving, as it does, three diverse participants with different motivations and understanding of the schemes. This raises the question of how easy or possible is it to overcome problems which may be intrinsic to such a complex system. Given the level of satisfaction with the arrangements for direct payments, perhaps the best thing would be to disturb them as little as possible. However, it is worth investigating what changes or improvements to the current system might mitigate the problems identified.

Changes and improvements

The main scope for improvement to the current system lies in improving the information given to those who use direct payments for paying arrears. Those using direct payments, money advisers and some of the creditors we interviewed commented on the need for better, more easily understood, regular information on amounts being deducted and arrears left to pay. The consumer is ultimately responsible for paying for consumption but depends on the creditor to give information of the amount to be paid and on the Benefits Agency to say what has been deducted from benefit and paid to the creditor. Problems arise when the amount to be paid changes, as in the case of changes in fuel consumption. Given the tight budgets of most people on Income Support and the evidence that they manage on a weekly basis, there is a case for regular statements, perhaps once every month, from the Benefits Agency to the user of a direct payment on the amount being deducted from benefit, and a statement from each creditor of their account, current consumption and arrears outstanding. A monthly statement has been suggested because it is an interval between the budgeting period of people on Income Support and the quarterly billing cycle of the fuel companies. At present consumers receive the regulation quarterly account, but in the interval between accounts might have built up further arrears. A three-monthly statement seems to be too infrequent and weekly would be too costly.

If regular statements were to be sent from the Benefits Agency on the deductions for direct payment, this could coincide with more regular review of direct payment cases to check for mistakes and delays in payments. Although this would inevitably require administrative resources, it is not necessarily a high-cost option. It would involve sending a standard letter triggered by the computer regularly if the Income Support recipient had a direct payment. More regular reviews of direct payment cases might be regarded as worthwhile in their own right. Those with direct payments for arrears could be considered to be among the more 'at risk' people on Income Support. This does not necessarily apply to those with direct payments for mortgage interest.

Clearly, the provision of monthly statements and additional reviews would have resource implications for the Benefits Agency which already offers the direct payments service free to eligible applicants and to creditors.

Other improvements which could be undertaken by the Benefits Agency in the administration of direct payments fall into two groups: those which are more or less internal to the Agency and those which affect relationships with creditors. One possible internal change, the integration of the computer system, is already under way. Improved computer networks would facilitate the introduction of targets to control delays and mistakes, and would help more regular reviews of direct payment cases to be undertaken. One way to decrease the likelihood of mistakes is to ensure that all adjudication officers and certainly all local offices have current copies of the guidelines and information leaflets on direct payment procedures. Some Benefits Agency staff had not seen these and were not aware of their existence as noted in Chapter Three. Information on appeals and redress in the case of direct payment is available in the IS9 leaflet but few staff or recipients appeared to know about it.

We have suggested that users of direct payment schemes are most vulnerable when they change address or when the amount of direct payment changes. An extreme example of this is when a direct payment finishes, usually when arrears have been paid off or when Income Support ceases on starting a job, for example. At this point it might be beneficial to offer a money advice service. If those who have cleared their debt and finished direct payments subsequently fall into arrears again because of lack of money advice at the appropriate time, they might have to start direct payments again. It is administratively inefficient and costly to stop and start direct payments. Those who start low-paid work are equally vulnerable and do not have the option of direct payments within Income Support. A money advice service could be provided within the Benefits Agency internally or could be provided by existing agencies such as Citizens Advice Bureaux or other established money advice agencies. If provided by the Benefits Agency, it would contribute to its commitment to provide effective information, and to its core values of improving services to the public and of increasing financial efficiency. Money advice is already part of the service offered within the administration of the Social Fund, and part of the training of Social Fund officers. This training could be extended to include selected people working in the direct payments section of local offices. Likewise, money advice is already provided by a range of outside agencies. Extending their services to advice concerning direct payments would not involve new function but could increase their workload

An administrative change proposed by creditors is that there should be one regional contact in the Benefits Agency for liaison about direct payments. At present some local authorities, for example, have to deal with a number of local Benefits Agency offices and each may have a different system for administering direct payments. This proposal might be difficult to accommodate within the present structure of the Benefits Agency based on district offices and Area Directorates. However, it could make the information exchange required for the smooth running of the direct payment system more satisfactory.

Of the changes which relate more directly to creditors, the scheduling of priorities for direct payments has perhaps caused more controversy than others. This has mainly been highlighted since the privatisation of water supplies. The water companies feel strongly about being fourth in the list of priorities for direct payment after electricity, gas and rent. If someone on Income Support is in arrears with water charges and they already have three higher priority payments a direct payment cannot be used to clear the arrears for water. However, only a small proportion (4 per cent) of those with any deduction have three or more deductions, so this problem might only occur in relatively few cases.

There are also other options for prioritising direct payments. First, the flat rate payment of £2.20 per week takes no account of the size of the arrears, so a small debt is paid off at a much quicker rate than a large one. It has been suggested that *pro rata* payments of debt, similar to those used when an administration order is made through the courts, would be a fairer representation of the demands of creditors (Ford, 1992). One of the main problems with this arrangement, however, is the need for constant adjustment of the payments to each creditor. This would mean regular recalculation of the direct payment by the Benefits Agency, and creditors would be less clear how much money they were getting at any given time. It has been pointed out that the direct payment set amount of £2.20 per week is one of its strong points. Also a constantly changing system would increase the chances of mistakes (PUAF, 1991).

A second option for altering the prioritising of direct payments is to give the user the choice of which payment they would prefer to pay by direct payment and for which they would be prepared to seek an alternative method of payment. This option fits well with the priorities of consumer choice and independence which is promoted in much government policy. Such an option might be more administratively complex than the present system. On the other hand, if a priority, once chosen, remained in force for that recipient, there might be little additional complexity.

One of the areas which has been shown to cause difficulty is the estimation of current consumption particularly for fuel direct. In return for the security of payment of arrears by direct payments guaranteed by the Benefits Agency, fuel companies could be asked to monitor the consumption of those on direct payments more regularly, and give monthly statements of their current consumption together with the monthly statement of the amount of arrears still owing. Monitoring the consumption of people on fuel direct links also with ideas of targeting this population for information and advice on energy efficiency and insulation measures through the Home Energy Efficiency Scheme (see Brady and Hutton, 1993).

Since the privatisation of the utilities, the secondary function of direct payments as a debt collecting service raises the question whether the Benefits Agency should operate a free service to a profit-making private business. Thus the charging of creditors for this service has become a policy option to be considered. At present mortgage lenders pay a charge for having mortgage interest payments transferred directly by the Benefits Agency. An extension of this principle to other creditors, such as fuel and water companies, could be examined.

Structural changes

Reduction of direct payment schemes

One of the reasons for the change from Supplementary Benefit to Income Support was the increasing complexity of Supplementary Benefit. Income Support was designed to be a simple benefit with premiums for particular groups such as pensioners, disabled people and lone parents replacing the large range of additional requirements. There is a case to be made for saying that the increasing numbers using direct payments and the corresponding rise in administrative costs should be controlled, and the number and type of direct payments should therefore be reduced. To some extent the numbers using direct payments could fall anyway. Increased use of pre-payment meters has meant a reduction in payments for electricity. Gas and water payments may follow suit. Payments for the Community Charge will eventually disappear. The structure of the new Council Tax and its general acceptability (compared with the Community Charge) will possibly mean fewer direct payments for Council Tax arrears in the future. Although obligatory direct payments for mortgage interest have been introduced relatively recently, the circumstances which required their introduction may change. The need for all Income Support recipients to have mortgage interest paid direct could reduce.

In the short run however, there appears to be a continuing need for each of the direct payment schemes and any reduction by discontinuing particular types of payment does not seem to be a feasible option. Other options might be more possible such as increasing the level of arrears which qualify for access to a direct payment or only making them available to particular categories of recipient such as lone parents, or unemployed people with children. Restricting the availability of direct payments only to families with children would have a direct and possibly severe effect on claimants in other categories. Although families with children are more likely to be in debt than other types of household, other claimants do face the possibility of eviction and disconnection. Direct payments are already schemes of last resort so there does not seem to be much scope for reduction in this way.

Both direct payments and deductions from benefit have implications for the amount of income left to the recipient for food and other everyday expenses. We have shown, not surprisingly, that the total amount of benefit deducted (whether for payment or recovery) increases with the number of deductions. Also the longer people are on Income Support, the more likely they are to have three or more deductions. It might be appropriate to consider in greater depth the circumstances of people who have been on Income Support for a long time and have accumulated a number of direct payments and deductions.

Abolition of direct payments

Taking the idea of reducing the direct payment system to its logical conclusion leads to the option of abolishing it altogether. Though extreme, there are arguments for abolishing direct payments from Income Support. They can be considered to be a legacy from more paternalistic times. The discretion allowed to adjudication officers to impose direct payments 'in the best interests of the family' takes away from claimants the responsibility and choice in deciding how the interests of their families are best served. There was always a tension within Supplementary Benefit between providing an overall amount of money for people to use as they chose and identifying amounts for particular items. Identification of the 'notional fuel element' within Supplementary Benefit and Income Support has long been a source of contention. The DSS deny that such a thing exists but lobbying organisations use historical evidence to trace the amount allowed for fuel expenditure in Supplementary Benefit. Direct payments for specific items sit uneasily within the principle of providing an income for people to spend as they wish. More recent ideas of consumer choice and independence, embodied in the Citizen's Charter, are also undermined by the intervention of the DSS to distribute recipients' money for them.

If direct payments were abolished, those on Income Support who use them and creditors would have to make alternative payment arrangements. However, there would be a risk that larger numbers than at present would be made homeless by eviction or repossession or be disconnected from water and fuel supplies. Distraint of goods or even imprisonment could also be faced. In our research we investigated alternatives to direct payments. The initial reaction of many respondents was that if direct payments were not available they would not know if or how they would pay. Faced with the reality, however, some would find the money somehow and manage. Pre-payment meters are an obvious alternative to direct payments for electricity, gas and water, although there might be considerable difficulty in the short-term for gas and water since suitable meters are not widely available. A further disadvantage of pre-payment meters is that the cost of electricity obtained this way is greater than through other payment methods. Servicing a pre-payment meter costs the company more than administering a quarterly account and the standing charge for a meter reflects this. Access to tokens can also cause problems. Although pre-payment meters prevent people building up arrears, there are problems with people not having money to feed the meter and going without heat. Some families with young children, and elderly people, could be put at risk in very cold weather. However, the use of budget plans and other payment arrangements whilst requiring greater self-discipline, might obviate such problems.

The worst outcomes could be mitigated by curtailing the sanctions available to creditors. At present electricity and gas companies are legally restrained by the Code of Practice from disconnecting elderly people and families with young children on Income Support. Such restrictions could be extended to a wider range types of payment apart from electricity and gas. Other types of household apart from the elderly or families with young children are at risk if no water supply is available.

Expansion of direct payments

A contrasting option to reducing or abolishing the current system of direct payment schemes is to expand it. Our research has highlighted the limited access to the schemes, and creditors, money advisers, users and even Benefit Agency staff have all proposed various ways they would like to see the scheme expanded. The most common suggestion is that direct payments should be available to people in receipt of other benefits and particularly to those in receipt of Invalidity Benefit. Those with impaired heath are likely to be at risk if water, or heat in the home is not available.

Creditors could be required to accept a direct payment if it is agreed by the consumer and the Benefits Agency. At present some creditors, particularly electricity companies, refuse and insist on installing a pre-payment meter. Such a proposal runs counter to policies for less state intervention in company practices, and would require a certain determination to overcome the reluctance of private companies.

Another expansion frequently mentioned is to allow people to continue to pay for current consumption after the arrears have been cleared. This already happens in some circumstances and it might seem only fair to make it available to all. If payment for current consumption were allowed for those who had had a direct payment, the question would then arise about others on Income Support. They might also welcome the opportunity to use direct payments as a method of payment for fuel and water bills. The DSS stated policy at present, however, is that direct payments are not offered as a general method of payment.

Another option is to offer direct payments as a preventive service. At a minimal level this might make information about the schemes available to all on Income Support. If people were aware that direct payments were available when they were in arrears, they

LIVERPOOL JOHN MOORES UNIVERSITY
LEARNING SERVICES

might apply before reaching a crisis and avoid a great deal of worry and stress. However, this option conflicts with current policy that direct payments are a last resort and would have large resource implications if many more Income Support recipients used the schemes.

This idea is linked with making direct payments available to all on Income Support. If this were the case information about the schemes could become widely available, for recipients, for creditors and for local offices. The schemes would become part of the routine administration of Income Support and less of detached, minority activity. This might overcome the problems of information, but not those of cost.

A further way to expand the use of the schemes is to lower the level of qualifying arrears. The lower the level of arrears, the sooner they would be paid off, and with smaller deductions from benefit. The disadvantage of lowering the threshold might be that people are drawn into the schemes who do not really need them. The preventive value for those who would have used direct payments anyway should be set against this.

The schemes could be expanded to cover other debts. For example, direct payments could be made available for items such as telephone charges and television licences and payments. Though not essential in the same way as fuel and housing, these items are increasingly seen as an integral part of the social participation fundamental to the welfare of families. It could be argued that both telephones and televisions are particularly valuable to families with children who are most likely to use direct payment schemes.

It has often been stated that those on low incomes do not have access to the same banking services as most other people. Loans and direct debit and preparation of statements of incomings and outgoings are what most of the population are used to and without which would find managing their budget difficult. The makings of a banking service are emerging within the benefit system in the operations of the Social Fund which offers loans, and in the system of direct payments which offer a direct debit system for some people on Income Support. Instead of offering direct payments in specific circumstances, there might be an argument for setting up more universal banking services for low-income households. State backing is likely to be necessary as private sources are unlikely to offer such a service. For example, in France and The Netherlands there are government subsidies to the private sector to fund social loans (Tester, 1987). The development and expansion of Credit Unions would be a further alternative. Credit Unions are local voluntary organisations which provide low-cost banking services including loans to those on low incomes. With additional support these services, including the option of offering direct debit services, could be expanded.

Choice versus imposition

At present mortgage interest direct payments are generally compulsory, as are payments for unpaid fines and for Community Charge arrears. Some payments for other items can also be initiated by the adjudication officer 'in the family's best interest'. One of the main arguments for not being too concerned about such lack of choice is that those who use direct payments do not mind. Our findings have shown that even when people did not choose a direct payment they were usually pleased with the arrangement. At a very basic level, concern has been expressed by some Benefits Agency staff that recipients are not always asked for consent when it is proposed to impose a direct payment. Imposition of direct payments in this way seems to run counter to the aim of independence which the benefit system attempts to promote.

There are a number of conditions governing when an adjudication officer can implement a direct payment without the recipient's consent. For example, a direct payment can be imposed if a claimant refuses consent but the adjudication officer nevertheless decides that the family's interest is best protected in this way. Also, imposition for payment of Community Charge arrears is similar to the attachment of earnings for defaulters who are in paid employment. It is a tax, and deduction from income at source for payment of tax through PAYE has long been accepted. Payment of mortgage interest direct has a parallel in Housing Benefit, but the justification for *imposing* direct payments for mortgage may not be equally valid. Although some are at risk of repossession, many people with a direct payment for mortgage interest feel they can manage their money and do not welcome the intervention of the DSS. Since some people will wish to use direct payments while others will prefer to pay themselves, this seems to be an area where choice could be returned to the consumer.

Other possibilities for choice have been mentioned earlier, in the option to continue with current payments after the debt has been cleared, and for recipients to choose the priority of payment. Making direct payments available to all on Income Support, that is making them available on demand, is a considerable widening of choice.

Summary

In this chapter we have considered a range of possible changes to the system of direct payments at present in operation. After considering whether or not direct payments should be continued we reviewed some administrative changes which would improve the system. In the second section we set out some more structural changes.

LIVERPOOL JOHN MOORES UNIVERSITY
Aldham Robarts L.R.C.
TEL. 051 231 3701/3634

Chapter 9   Summary and Conclusion

In this research we have reviewed the operation and use of the range of direct payment schemes which form part of the Income Support system. These schemes have attracted a considerable amount of public debate and have been the subject of consultation and negotiation between organisations representing claimants' interests, creditors and the Department of Social Security. In view of this we have adopted a pluralistic approach to data collection and analysis.

Specifically our research aims were to provide information on the following:

- the numbers, types and levels of direct payment in operation

- the factors which lead people to be put on direct payments, their usefulness, and the consequences of being refused or of coming off direct payments

- the views and practices of third-party creditors, and

- how staff in social security offices administer the direct payments regulations.

In addressing these issues we have sought the views and experiences of Income Support recipients through a national survey and in-depth interviews in three areas of England. Information on current practices and views about direct payments were collected from creditors, creditor organisations, money advice agencies and regulatory bodies using face-to-face interviews, telephone interviews and documentary analysis. The views and experiences of Benefits Agency office staff were collected in interviews during fieldwork visits.

In the rest of this chapter we start by summarising the main empirical findings of the research and identify the most important issues arising from them. Following this we discuss the policy options that the DSS might consider in the future.

Summary of findings

The analysis of ASE data between May 1991 and August 1993 presented in Chapter Two illustrates well the dynamic nature of the use of direct payments. At a time when the general numbers of people receiving Income Support has been rising, it not surprising to find the numbers on direct payments also increasing. However, the actual increase in the number of direct payments in the years 1991–93 (from 486,000 to 1,628,000) has also reflected changes both within and outside the benefit system. For example, the decision to pay mortgage interest direct to lenders largely contributed to an increase in mortgage direct payments from 8,000 in May 1991 to 371,000 in August 1993. The general increase in the price of water following privatisation led to a rise in the number of people in arrears to the water companies. This has fed through to an increase in the number of direct payments for water. The introduction of the Community Charge also created large numbers of people falling into arrears, which again is reflected in the rise in direct payments from 58,000 to 555,000 by August 1993. By contrast, the increases in the numbers of people on fuel or rent direct are more modest.

Although over 800,000 direct payments were being made in May 1992, a relatively small proportion of the whole Income Support population was affected. For example, fewer than five per cent of all recipients were making payments for Community Charge arrears, fewer than four per cent for gas, and fewer than three per cent each for water, electricity and rent. Of those with direct payments the most frequent users were lone parents and unemployed people. While the majority of Income Support recipients have only one deduction from their benefit at any one time, there is a tendency for the number of deductions to increase with the length of time a person is on benefit.

The process of coming onto a direct payment scheme was, for most people, a straightforward exercise. The relatively low levels of knowledge about the schemes are partly a reflection of the conscious policy of the DSS to provide information only at the point of need, in keeping with the view of direct payments as a system of last resort. Whilst there was evidence of a potentially greater need for direct payments (from the numbers of respondents in our survey who reported financial difficulties) we did not discover a large degree of unmet demand (relatively few respondents not already on direct payments thought they might want to use the service).

When on direct payments the large majority of survey respondents said they were satisfied, even when the payments had been imposed. They liked the security that direct payments offered (of fuel and water supply, and of keeping a roof over their heads) and the way it helped them to manage their finances. Those with mobility or other access problems particularly appreciated the automatic payment of their bills. The main problem or complaint from users was the lack of adequate information about their payments, particularly when these had been imposed.

Direct payments have a different aim from other types of deduction from benefit and can be treated separately in the development of policy. However, such a distinction is largely irrelevant for Income Support recipients. For them it is the *cumulative* effect of all types of deduction that is important. Hence, one of the criticisms of direct deductions (that is, direct payments and deductions for Social Fund loans and overpayments) is that people are often left with little remaining income to live on. The evidence from our survey (reported in Chapter Four) is that a minority, 40 per cent of the 309 people on direct deductions, described themselves as having enough to live on after deductions. At first this appears to be inconsistent with the finding that most users find direct payments helpful. However, the two findings are not necessarily contradictory and may, in contrast, reflect that direct payments ameliorate the general difficulties of living on a low income.

For some Income Support recipients, coming off direct payments causes difficulties. The advantages of direct payments and the budgeting discipline that they automatically impose are not always easy to recreate with other methods of payment. The result in some cases is a return to debt and to direct payments. For others, regaining direct control of their finances is both welcome and unproblematic. For these people direct payments have served the useful purpose of helping them deal successfully with a temporary problem of indebtedness.

The attitudes of creditors to direct payments vary. For some electricity companies in particular they are used as a system of last resort when other payment methods are not possible. For other creditors they are one of a number of methods of payment to be used when appropriate. Whilst there were several suggestions for improving the administrative efficiency of direct payments (and some complaints from water companies about the priority ordering) we found widespread support and acceptance of the schemes in principle. There was a degree of concern, however, at the tendency of some people to increase their consumption of gas and electricity once on direct payments beyond their capacity to pay.

Like third-party creditors, Benefits Agency staff were also able to point to a number of changes in the administration of direct payments which they felt would improve the service they provide. Problems concerned with the transfer of information internally, and between Benefits Agency offices and outside parties are known to the DSS, and are being addressed by, for example, integrating mainframe and microcomputer systems. Most decision making on direct payment applications seemed to cause little difficulty for the adjudication officers interviewed during the study. The relevant regulations are generally clear cut. Where there is scope for judgement or discretion on the part of an adjudication officer, for example, in the interpretation of 'in the interests of the claimant or the family' there are clear guidelines in the Adjudication Officer's Guide. There was, however, some suggestion that the workload of the office was sometimes a factor in decisions about whether to continue direct payments for current consumption after arrears had been paid off.

The general conclusion to emerge from our empirical analysis, which we state at the beginning of Chapter Eight, is that direct payment schemes are useful for large numbers of Income Support recipients and generally supported by third-party creditors. However, there are a number of ways in which the schemes could be altered to adapt to the recent changes in their range and their use. These are summarised in the next section.

Future policy towards direct payments

The future policy towards direct payments will depend upon how their functions are viewed. As we have described earlier, the original aim of direct payments was to be a system of last resort, a means of preventing creditor sanctions which would have serious consequences for the welfare of Income Support recipients. So, fuel and water direct were intended to prevent disconnection of essential utilities, and rent direct to prevent eviction by a local authority. The expansion of direct payments, to Community Charge arrears and unpaid fines, can be seen as a continuation of this last resort approach. Again the aim is to prevent the serious sanctions of repossession, seizure of goods and imprisonment.

We have argued in Chapter Eight that abolishing the range of direct payment schemes would neither benefit users nor meet with the approval of third-party creditors. The evidence that large numbers of Income Support recipients still accrue arrears for fuel, water and rent and the increase in the types of direct payments in operation, provide a strong indication that there will be a continued need for direct payments in the future.

Although there are opportunities to change the *structure* of the direct payment schemes (which are summarised below) there are also a number of improvements which the Benefits Agency could make within the existing structure which would retain the underlying last resort approach. Some of these changes (which are discussed fully in Chapter Eight) are of a mainly administrative nature and include the following:

- more comprehensive and regular information for people with direct payments, for example on amounts being deducted and the amounts of arrears outstanding

- more effective information on the availability of direct payments for potential users, and on appeal rights for refused applicants

- the introduction of targets for clearance times and appropriate performance indicators to ensure efficient processing of cases.

Other changes possible within the current structure which would enhance the preventive role of direct payments include:

- the provision of money advice (by the Benefits Agency or existing money advice agencies) for people applying for, or about to come off, direct payments

- reducing the qualifying times and amounts of arrears so that people can be accepted on to direct payments earlier

- increasing the maximum number of direct payments to four or five

- introducing a *pro rata* payment regime which divides the amount of money a person can afford between creditors according to the size of each debt.

Third-party creditors could also contribute to improving the service to direct payment users. Although we suggest above that the Benefits Agency could provide more information for people on direct payments, it may be more appropriate for creditors to undertake this. In addition, the utilities could provide more frequent and accurate estimations of current consumption.

Although direct payments are seen as a measure of last resort by the DSS, our evidence shows that some benefit recipients and creditors use them differently. Direct payments are valued not only because they prevent serious sanctions, but also because they are a useful aid to household budgeting for people and a reliable method of arrears recovery for creditors. In other words direct payments are valued because they address the needs of benefit recipients and creditors beyond the prevention of final sanctions.

The way in which direct payments are actually used and valued by Income Support recipients suggests an alternative to the last resort approach which would have a wider range of policy implications to those described above. Direct payments could be offered to recipients of other benefits who may experience similar problems with arrears or budgeting as Income Support recipients. Furthermore, direct payments could be seen as a freely-available service to benefit recipients to enable them to pay their bills as they wish. We have already described the policy developments that are possible while still retaining the current structure based on direct payments as a system of last resort. All of these policy options would remain relevant under the alternative view of direct payments as a freely-available service, but there are two further policy implications which could also follow. First, the power to impose direct payments and, more generally, the duty of adjudication officers to make decisions about the best interests of people and their families would become inappropriate. Direct payments would only be implemented on a request from a benefit recipient (subject to the creditor's agreement). Secondly, direct payments would be available for the payment of all bills (including others which are not part of the current range, such as for telephone and television charges), and not only those with arrears attached.

When used as an aid to budgeting, direct payments come to resemble direct debits from bank accounts. Both ensure that bills are paid regularly at an appropriate amount and spread the burden of payment evenly throughout the year. However, paying by direct debit is only available for those with bank or building society accounts (which would exclude over half the people in our survey). Also there are important distinctions between direct debits and direct payments. The former are offered as a comprehensive service to account holders and not restricted to those who have accumulated arrears. It is for customers to choose whether or not to use the service. By contrast, direct payments can only be made when arrears have accrued and are subject to the provision that they are necessary for the interests of the family. The final decision therefore rests with a DSS adjudication officer and not the Income Support recipient. They can also be imposed, again on the decision of an adjudication officer. The similarities and differences between direct payments and direct debits, and the recognition that Income Support already serves some quasi-banking functions for some benefit recipients suggest the far-reaching policy idea, raised in the previous chapter, of introducing state-backed universal banking services for low-income households. A less ambitious alternative to this might be the expansion of existing Credit Unions which already provide low-cost banking services to people on low incomes.

Direct payments as a last resort and as a freely-available service are not of course mutually exclusive options but should be seen as opposite ends of a continuum between which elements of both can happily co-exist. Indeed, within the existing last resort approach the provisions for paying for current consumption of fuel and water after arrears are paid off can be seen as moving slightly towards the freely-available end of the continuum.

An alternative direction for policy is not to expand the services available but to introduce restrictions in order to target them more effectively or to reduce the cost of administration. Options discussed in the previous chapter include increasing the level of accrued arrears before a recipient becomes eligible for direct payments, and limiting access to families with young children.

A final policy option is to charge creditors for the use of the direct payment service. The arguments for and against charging are well known to the DSS and this study was not intended to advance the debate any further. What is clear, however, is that it would not be in the interests of Income Support recipients to pursue this policy if a likely outcome was some creditors withdrawing from the schemes or passing on the cost to their customers through higher bills.

Concluding discussion

The recent dynamic nature of direct payments is set to continue for a number of reasons, both internal and external to the schemes themselves. The large increases in the number of people on direct payments associated with external policy changes might be expected to level off. In particular, Community Charge payments will eventually disappear (though this may take many years). New payments and deductions (child support and fines, for example) have been introduced and will create further temporary surges in the total number of people with direct payments (again until demand levels out). Increase in the demand for direct payments might also flow from two other recent policy changes. First, the imposition of VAT on fuel will lead to higher fuel bills which some people will find difficult to meet despite the compensation arrangements which came into effect in April 1994. Secondly, the introduction of Jobseeker's Allowance (lasting six months) to replace Unemployment Benefit (which was paid for twelve months) will increase the number of unemployed people on Income Support. Changes in alternative methods of paying bills will continue as creditors adjust their policies to their own internal imperatives and to the possibilities created by developments in technology. Opportunities of paying bills by direct debit will increase as more benefit recipients take up the option of receiving their benefits through Automated Credit Transfer (ACT).

The future policy on direct payments must have regard not only to these developments but also to the pressures on, and tensions within the system. For example, direct payments are useful for benefit recipients and in most cases make life easier for them. They are also useful for creditors. However, to improve the lot of one group, by, for example, relaxing or tightening the levels of repayment, might adversely affect the other. The introduction of greater elements of compulsion in direct payments (for example, through mortgage direct and child maintenance) reduces the opportunity for people to exercise financial independence and control (at the heart of much social security and other government policy in recent years). The rationale of direct payments as a system of last resort does not match their actual use as budgeting devices by benefit recipients. A consumer-led response to this would produce an expansion of direct payment schemes. However, the DSS gains no direct benefit from providing the service but instead incurs considerable administrative costs which would increase further if any expansion took place.

In some ways these pressures and tensions are the price of success. But they also demonstrate a need for the continuation of the current direct payment schemes, at least in the medium-term, and point to opportunities for promoting greater consumer choice for benefit recipients and for control over their finances and welfare. Nevertheless, whether or not there are changes in the general policy towards direct payments, the administration of the schemes could undoubtedly be improved in the ways which we have outlined, to the benefit of both Income Support recipients and creditors.

Appendix 1 The Qualitative Interviews

The qualitative element of the research involved interviewing Income Support recipients, Benefits Agency staff, money advisers, and third parties. The interviews were conducted between April and July 1993 in three areas. These areas were selected to represent a broad range of local Benefits Agency office workloads and chosen from the same sampling frame used for a parallel project examining changes in circumstances:

- area 1 covers a large metropolitan city in the North of England

- area 2 covers a London Borough

- area 3 covers a medium sized town in the Midlands of England.

Interviews with recipients

We interviewed 15 Income Support recipients in each of the three areas. These interviews were conducted at recipients' homes, and generally lasted between 30 and 45 minutes. All interviews were tape-recorded and later transcribed.

Interviews were based on a topic guide, although the interview structure was sufficiently flexible for respondents to raise any additional issues that were important to them. A copy of the topic guide is contained in Appendix Two.

The broad issues covered by the interviews included how useful direct payments are for recipients, problems with coming on to and coming off direct payments, attitudes towards imposition, and consequences for applicants who are refused direct payments.

The sample was drawn from the case-records of three local district offices. We asked staff in each of the three offices to draw a sample of 30 recipients. Each of these samples were to include recipients who covered the full range of direct payments, all claimant types and recipients who were currently using direct payments, those who had been refused direct payments and people who had come off direct payments. Having identified a sample of 30 people in each area, these people were then contacted by letter requesting them to reply by freephone if they did not wish to be included in the research. Only five out of the 90 recipients contacted declined to be included in the research. In each area, the researchers interviewed 15 recipients who had not earlier indicated that they wished to withdraw from the study.

In area 1 we interviewed five unemployed recipients, five lone parents, two disabled people and three pensioners. Of these, 11 were currently using direct payments, two had been refused and two had come off direct payments.

In area 2 we interviewed four unemployed recipients, four lone parents, three disabled people and four pensioners. Of these ten were currently using direct payments, two had been refused and three had come off direct payments.

In area 3 we interviewed five unemployed recipients, four lone parents, three disabled people, and three pensioners. Of these 11 were currently using direct payments, two had been refused and two had come off direct payments.

Interviews with Benefits Agency staff

We conducted interviews with staff from a district office in each of the three areas. We interviewed supervisors and staff at LO1 and LO2 level, involved with the administration of direct payments. These interviews were based on a topic guide, (see Appendix

Two). The issues covered in these interviews included, staff views of the positive and negative aspects of direct payments, the decision making criteria used by adjudication officers to continue or reject applications for direct payments, and the relationship with third parties.

Interviews with third parties

We conducted in each area interviews with senior and middle managers from a variety of third parties. These interviews were based on a topic guide, (see Appendix Two). The issues covered in these interviews included the financial costs and benefits of direct payment schemes to third parties, their relationship with the Benefits Agency, and the alternative methods of payment available.

In area 1 we interviewed staff from British Gas, the regional electricity and water companies, as well as the local council concerning rent and Community Charge arrears. In area 2 we interviewed staff from British Gas, and the regional electricity company. In area 3 we interviewed staff from British Gas, the regional electricity and water companies. In addition we also interviewed the under secretary of the Council for Mortgage Lenders.

Interviews with money advisers

In each of the three areas we interviewed two money advisers from local Citizens Advice Bureaux. These interviews were based on a topic guide, (see Appendix Two). The issues covered in these interviews included the positive and negative aspects of direct payments, and the financial and social welfare implications of alternative payment methods.

Appendix 2   Qualitative Interviews: Topic Guides

Recipients

1. Current use of direct payment schemes
    * knowledge of schemes
    * whose decision to seek direct payments

2. Level of arrears and attitudes to debt
    * patterns of debt
    * causes of debt
    * other payment methods sought
    * stage in arrears cycle when direct payments and alternative payment methods sought

3. Usefulness of direct payments
    * are direct payments useful
    * why are they useful
    * how could they be more useful

4. Problems with direct payments
    * reasons why direct payments cause problems
    * information/administrative problems
    * budgeting problems
    * attitudes to imposition
    * availability on demand
    * level of remaining benefit

5. Attitudes and implications of non-acceptance

6. Attitudes and implications of coming off direct payments

Creditors

1. Financial costs and benefits of direct payments
    * costs of debt recovery (alternative forms)
    * administrative costs of processing direct payments

2. Alternative payment and debt recovery methods

3. Relationship with Benefits Agency
    * joint boards/meetings

LIVERPOOL JOHN MOORES UNIVERSITY
Aldham Roberts L.R.C.
TEL. 051 231 3701/3634

- staff perceptions of difficulties

4. Administration of direct payments

5. Impact of use of direct payments on the use of fuel

6. Views on alternatives to direct payments
   - attitudes towards priorities
   - number of deductions
   - ceiling on deductions
   - pro-rata distribution

Advice Agency staff

1. Positive aspects of direct payments

2. Problems associated with direct payments

3. Scale of consumer problems with direct payments

4. Relationship with Benefits Agency

5. Relationship with third parties

6. Solutions to improving the service

7. Financial and social implications of alternative payment/debt recovery methods

Benefits Agency staff

1. Positive aspects of direct payments

2. Problems for recipients when dealing with Benefits Agency and direct payments
   - do claimants understand the schemes
   - are they provided with adequate information
   - do recipients understand how direct payments are made
   - should direct payments be available on demand

3. Decision making criteria
   - eligibility for direct payments
   - interests of the family
   - continuing direct payments after debt paid

4. Methods of improving administration of direct payments

5. Relationship with third parties

6. Relationship with advice agencies

7. Alternatives to direct payments

Appendix 3 Data Sets Used in the Quantitative Analyses

The Annual Statistical Enquiry (ASE)

The ASE gathers information on a one per cent sample of recipients of Income Support in May each year. Information is available on the family composition of each recipient, whether a recipient is unemployed, a lone parent, a pensioner, or disabled. A recipient's use of direct payments and whether he or she has other deductions from Income Support are also available. Some analyses of this information are published each year, but for this study additional and more detailed analyses have been made available by DSS statisticians at the request of the researchers.

The SPRU national survey of Income Support recipients

A nationally representative sample of recipients of Income Support were interviewed in February and March 1993. The main purpose of the survey was to investigate the changes in circumstances occurring in a six-month interval. However some questions on the use of direct payments and deductions from Income Support, attitudes to managing money and methods of payment were also included in the survey. The fieldwork was undertaken by Research Services Limited (RSL).

A total of 1,137 achieved interviews was obtained, a response rate of 71 per cent. The aim was to interview 1,200 recipients of Income Support, approximately 40 from each of 30 Benefits Agency District offices. The offices were selected to represent the socio-demographic, geographical, and administrative variation among offices. Recipients were sampled according to the numbers in each local office and their likelihood of having experienced changes in circumstances. Pensioners were less likely to experience changes than other types of recipient so the sample was designed to under-sample pensioners. Analysis of the May 1991 ASE was used to determine the appropriate proportions of pensioners. However, in the interval between the interviews and this analysis unemployment had risen and the relative proportion of pensioners on Income Support had fallen. Thus the proportions selected corresponded closely to the current distribution of different types of recipients, as seen in Table 1. So to obtain population estimates it is not necessary to weight the sample results.

Table 1 Comparison of achieved interviews with distribution of claimant types in November 1992

Type of recipient	May 1991 ASE	Proportion with changes	Addresses submitted to RSL	Achieved interviews		November 1992 QSE†
	%	%	%	N	%	%
Pensioners	35	25	26	338	30	31
Disabled	8	15	8	130	11	9
Lone parents	19	20	18	216	19	18
Unemployed	30	30	38	403	35	35
Other	7	11	8	50	4	8

† The Quarterly Statistical Enquiry (QSE) is similar but not so detailed as the ASE

The Family Expenditure Survey (FES)

The FES is a national household survey of income and expenditure. The FES proved to be unsuitable as the question about whether direct payments are used in paying for fuel has been discontinued since 1988. Considerable changes to the direct payment schemes have taken place since then so the value of any analysis of the 1988 FES as a guide to current use is questionable. Checking with Central Statistical Office about whether any questions were asked about direct payments revealed that interviewers were asked to find out if any payments were made direct and these were added to expenditure information. By the 1991 FES, however, a question was included on whether any items of household expenditure had been paid directly by someone outside the household, including the DSS. This information is only available in the raw data set and not in the derived data set which is the one most readily accessible to researchers. It is not clear from the variable list that direct payments by the DSS will be easily separated from other expenditures paid directly by someone outside the household. Nor is it obvious what such an analysis would add to the information we now have from the national sample of Income Support recipients.

The PSI survey of credit and debt

The PSI study is a rich source of information on financial management. In 1989 a representative national sample of households in Britain and Northern Ireland was interviewed about their use of and attitudes to credit, about their money management and about the amount of debt they had. From a total sample of 2,212 households interviewed, 324 were on Income Support and 62 in the unweighted sample had deductions from benefit to pay third-party creditors and for recovery by the DSS for Social Fund loans and overpayments. Those likely to be in debt were oversampled and this group will include those with deductions from benefit. When weighted to compensate for oversampling the numbers of households with deductions from benefit becomes quite small. However, as we were not interested in preparing population estimates, but in those with deductions from benefit and in comparisons with those without deductions, it was appropriate to use the unweighted sample. With only 62 cases with direct deductions complex analysis proved to be inappropriate, but some interesting results were obtained on differences in attitudes to credit and debt between those with direct payments and others on Income Support. A data set of information on the recipients of Income Support included in the survey was prepared by PSI for analysis by researchers in SPRU.

Appendix 4   Direct Payments Section of the Changes in Circumstances Questionnaire

Deductions for direct payments questions

Q.800   I'd like to ask you now about any deductions that are made from your benefit. Sometimes the DSS takes money off people's benefit for various things, such as fuel or water bills, rent, and poll tax bills. This is often with the agreement of the claimant but their agreement is not always necessary. Did you know there were such schemes?

YES 1 – **Q.801**

NO 2 – **Q.822**

Q.801   Please look at this list and say if you have any money taken off for any of them at the moment OR have had at any time since 1 August/DATE AT Q.102. **CODE ALL THAT APPLY**

NONE	00	**Q.814**
GAS	01	
ELECTRICITY	02	
WATER	03	
RENT	04	
MORTGAGE	05	
OVERPAYMENT OF BENEFIT	06	
COMMUNITY CHARGE (POLL TAX) ARREARS	07	
PAYMENT OF FINE(S)	08	
SOCIAL FUND REPAYMENT	09	
OTHER (SPECIFY)	88	

ASK Q.802 – Q.813 FOR EACH DEDUCTION MENTIONED AT Q.801

Q.802   When did you start having deductions made for (DEDUCTION)?
ENTER DATE

ALLOW DK
DO NOT ALLOW REF/NULL

ASK Q.803 FOR CODES 1, 2 OR 3 AT Q.801 ONLY

Q.803   What was the main reason for the deduction being made originally?
READ OUT

PAY OFF ARREARS	1
PAY FOR CURRENT CONSUMPTION	2
PAY FOR ARREARS AND CURRENT CONSUMPTION	3

ALLOW DK
DO NOT ALLOW REF/NULL

Q.803a   Did you have any choice in the decision to have this deduction made, or was the decision imposed upon you?

HAD SOME CHOICE	1 –	**Q.804**

IMPOSED	2 –	**Q.805**
OTHER (SPECIFY)	3 –	**Q.805**
DON'T KNOW	9 –	**Q.805**

DO NOT ALLOW REF/NULL

Q.804　Did *you* request the DSS to make a deduction from your benefit for (DEDUCTION) or did the suggestion come from somewhere else?
PROMPT FOR WHERE SUGGESTION CAME FROM

RESPONDENTS IDEA	1	**SKIP TO Q.806**

CREDITOR (FUEL/WATER CO./ LANDLORD)	2	
DSS	3	
MONEY ADVISER	4	**ASK Q.805**
FRIEND/RELATIVE	5	
OTHER	6	

DO NOT ALLOW DK/REF/NULL

Q.805　To what extent did you agree with the idea? Would you say you agreed...**READ OUT**

VERY WILLINGLY	1
WILLINGLY	2
NOT VERY WILLINGLY	3
NOT AT ALL WILLINGLY	4

DO NOT ALLOW DK/REF/NULL

Q.806　How much was being taken off each week *originally*?
ENTER AMOUNT. ALLOW £00.00p – £99.99p

ALLOW DK
DO NOT ALLOW NULL/REF

Q.807　Are you still having money taken off for (DEDUCTION)?

YES 1 – **Q.810**
NO 2 – **Q.808**

ALLOW DK ROUTE TO Q.812a
DO NOT ALLOW REF/NULL

Q.808　What date did the deduction stop?
ENTER DATE

ALLOW DK
DO NOT ALLOW REF/NULL

Q.809　What was the *main* reason the deduction stopped?
CODE ONE ONLY.

PAID OFF ARREARS	1
CAME OFF INCOME SUPPORT	2
SWITCHED TO OTHER FORM OF PAYMENT	3
FUEL BOARD/COUNCIL STOPPED PAYMENT	4
DSS STOPPED PAYMENT	5
COULDN'T AFFORD PAYMENTS/ NEEDED THE MONEY	6

OTHER   8
DON'T KNOW   9

NOW ASK Q.812a

ASK IF CODED 1, 2 OR 3 AT Q.801

Q.810   At the moment is the deduction being used to ... **READ OUT CODE ONE ONLY**

PAY OFF ARREARS OF A BILL ONLY	1
PAY FOR CURRENT CONSUMPTION ONLY	2
PAY FOR ARREARS AND CURRENT CONSUMPTION	3

ALLOW DK
DO NOT ALLOW REF/NULL

Q.811   How much is being take off each week *now*?
ENTER AMOUNT £00.00p – £99.99p

ALLOW DK
DO NOT ALLOW REF/NULL

Q.812   How much of the arrears have you left to pay off?
ENTER AMOUNT £00.00p – £99999.99p

ALLOW DK
DO NOT ALLOW REF/NULL

IF CODE 9 (SOCIAL FUND) AT Q.801 GO TO Q.813. OTHERS ASK Q.812a

Q.812a   How do you think you would have managed to pay for (DEDUCTION) if the money *wasn't* being taken off your benefit. **PROBE**: Would there have been any problems for you?
ENTER VERBATIM

ALLOW DK
DO NOT ALLOW REF/NULL

Q.813   How would you say having this deduction for (DEDUCTION) has affected your household budgeting?
CODE ONE ONLY

MADE THINGS MUCH WORSE	1
MADE THINGS A LITTLE WORSE	2
NO EFFECT EITHER WAY	3
MADE THINGS A BIT EASIER	4
MADE THINGS A LOT EASIER	5

ALLOW DK
DO NOT ALLOW REF/NULL

Q.813a   Overall, do you feel that having deductions from your benefit has left you enough money to live on? **READ OUT**

YES, DEFINITELY	1
YES, JUST ABOUT	2
NO, NOT QUITE ENOUGH	3
NO, DEFINITELY NOT ENOUGH	4

ALLOW DK
DO NOT ALLOW REF/NULL

ASK ALL

Q.814   Since 1 August/DATE AT Q.102 have you ever wanted to have some money deducted from your benefit for anything but were refused?

YES 1 – **ASK Q.815**
NO 2 – **SKIP TO Q.818**

DO NOT ALLOW DK/REF/NULL

Q.815   How many times were you refused?

ENTER 1 – 10

ASK Q.816 – Q.817a FIRST 2 REFUSALS

SHOW CARD M

Q.816   Thinking about the (next) most recent time that you were refused a direct deduction. What was the application for?
CODE ALL THAT APPLY

GAS	01
ELECTRICITY	02
WATER	03
RENT	04
MORTGAGE	05
OVERPAYMENT OF BENEFIT	06
COMMUNITY CHARGE (POLL TAX) ARREARS	07
MAINTENANCE PAYMENT	08
PAYMENT OF FINE(S)	09
SOCIAL FUND PAYMENT	10
OTHER (SPECIFY)	88

ALLOW DK
DO NOT ALLOW REF/NULL

Q.817   Why were you refused?
CODE ONE ONLY

FUEL BOARD WANTED OTHER FORM OF PAYMENT	1
ARREARS TOO LARGE	2
ARREARS TOO SMALL	3
AMOUNT OF BENEFIT TOO SMALL	4
OTHER DEDUCTIONS HAD PRIORITY	5
OTHER (SPECIFY)	8

ALLOW DK
DO NOT ALLOW REF/NULL

Q.817a   How did you deal with (DEDUCTION) after you were refused by the DSS?
ENTER VERBATIM

DO NOT ALLOW DK/REF/NULL

ALLOW ALL WHO HAVE HAD OR ARE HAVING OR WHO WERE REFUSED DEDUCTIONS (I.E. THOSE CODED 1 TO 9 AT Q.801 OR CODED 1 AT Q.814) OTHERS GO TO Q.822

Q.818   How did you *first* find out about deductions from benefit?
CODE ONE ONLY

CREDITOR (FUEL/WATER CO./ LANDLORD)	1
DSS	2
MONEY ADVISER	3
FRIEND/RELATIVE	4
OTHER	5

ALLOW DK
DO NOT ALLOW REF/NULL

ASK ALL

Q.822   Do you think these schemes are a good idea?

YES   1
NO   2   **Q.822a**

ALLOW DK
DO NOT ALLOW REF/NULL

Q.822a   Why do you say this?

PROBE FULLY
ENTER VERBATIM

ALLOW DK
DO NOT ALLOW REF/NUL

ASK IF NO (CODE 2) AT Q.822

Q.823   If you had known about the schemes earlier do you think you might have tried to get a deduction made for something?

YES 1 – **Q.824**

NO 2 – **Q.900**
DK 3

DO NOT ALLOW REF/NUL

Q.824   Which of these do you think you might have wanted to pay for by deductions from benefit?
CODE ALL THAT APPLY

GAS	1
ELECTRICITY	2
WATER	3
RENT	4
MORTGAGE	5
OVERPAYMENT OF BENEFIT	6
COMMUNITY CHARGE (POLL TAX) ARREARS	7
PAYMENT OF FINES	8
OTHER (SPECIFY)	9

ALLOW DK
DO NOT ALLOW REF/NULL

Appendix 5   Additional Questions Used from the Changes in Circumstances Questionnaire

Q.507b   How do you pay for electricity at the moment?

CODE ALL THAT APPLY

BILL PAID BY DIRECT DEBIT FROM A BANK/BUILDING SOCIETY ACCOUNT	1 –	**Q.507c**

BILL PAID BY CASH/CHEQUE	2 –	**Q.508**
DEDUCTION FROM INCOME SUPPORT	3 –	**Q.508**
PRE-PAYMENT METER	4 –	**Q.507e**
BUDGET SCHEME	5 –	**Q.508**
OTHER (SPECIFY)	6 –	**Q.508**

DO NOT ALLOW DK/REF/NULL

IF CODE 3 AT Q.507b

Q.507c   How would you describe the effect of paying by direct debit on your budgeting for electricity?

READ OUT LIST

VERY HELPFUL	1
QUITE HELPFUL	2
QUITE UNHELPFUL	3
VERY UNHELPFUL	4
NO EFFECT EITHER WAY	5

ALLOW DK
DO NOT ALLOW REF/NUL
NOW ASK Q.508

IF RESPONSE TO Q.507b WAS 4 (I.E. PRE-PAYMENT METER) ASK Q.507e

REST: SKIP TO Q.508

Q.507e   Did you choose to have a pre-payment meter or did the electricity company insist on you having one?

RESPONDENT'S OWN CHOICE	1 –	**Q.507h**

ELECTRICITY CO. INSISTED	2 –	**Q.507f**

DO NOT ALLOW DK/REF/NULL

Q.507f   At the time did you mind having a pre-payment meter installed?

YES, I DID MIND	1 –	**Q.507g**

NO, I DIDN'T MIND	2 –	**Q.507h**

DO NOT ALLOW DK/REF/NULL

Q.507g   How would you have preferred to pay instead of a pre-payment meter?

BILL PAID BY DIRECT DEBIT FROM A
BANK/BUILDING SOCIETY ACCOUNT   1
BILL PAID BY CASH/CHEQUE   2
DEDUCTION FROM INCOME SUPPORT   3
PRE-PAYMENT METER   4
BUDGET SCHEME   5
OTHER (SPECIFY)   8

Q.507h   What sort of pre-payment meter is it?

COIN OPERATED   1
TOKEN OPERATED   2
USES RECHARGEABLE KEY OR CARD   3

ALLOW DK
DO NOT ALLOW REF/NUL

Q.507j   Does the meter payment collect for ... **READ OUT**

CURRENT ELECTRICITY USE ONLY   1
CURRENT USE *AND* PAST ARREARS   2

ALLOW DK
DO NOT ALLOW REF/NULL

Q.507k   Have you ever been in the situation of wanting to use the electricity but not being able to?

YES 1 – **Q.507l**

NO 2 – **INSTRUCTION ABOVE Q.507m**

Q.507l   Can you tell me the reasons you couldn't use the electricity?

NOT ENOUGH MONEY (FOR METER/   1
TOKENS/KEY/CARD)
PLACE TO RECHARGE KEY/CARD   2
NOT OPEN
PLACE TO RECHARGE KEY/CARD   3
TOO FAR AWAY
CUT OFF FOR REPAIR   4
CUT OFF FOR NON-PAYMENT   5
OTHER (SPECIFY)   8

ALLOW DK
DO NOT ALLOW REF/NULL

INTERVIEWER: IF RESPONSE TO Q.507h WAS 2 OR 3, ASK Q.507m REST: ASK Q.507p

Q.507m   How far away is the place where you (buy tokens/recharge key or card)?
ENTER NUMBER OF MILES 0 to 50

IF LESS THEN ONE ENTER 0

ALLOW DK
DO NOT ALLOW REF/NULL

Q.507n   How long does it usually take to get there?
ENTER NUMBER OF HOURS AND MINUTES UP TO 3 HOURS

ALLOW DK
DO NOT ALLOW REF/NULL

Q.507p   Thinking about the month of January 1993, on how many days did (you have no money or tokens/your key or card run out)?
ENTER NUMBER OF DAYS 0 TO 31

ALLOW DK
DO NOT ALLOW REF/NULL

ASK ALL
Q.508   In any of the places you have lived since 1 August/DATE AT Q.102, including here, have you used gas?

YES 1 – **Q.507q**

NO 2 – **Q.514**

DO NOT ALLOW REF/NULL

Q.507q   Do you pay all or part of your gas costs?

YES 1 – **Q.508a**

NO 2 – **Q.514**
DK 3 –

DO NOT ALLOW REF/NULL

Q.508a   How many times, since 1 August/DATE AT Q.102, have there been any large changes to do with your gas, such as your bills, how you pay for gas, or with your gas supply?

ENTER NUMBER OF TIMES 0 – 99
IF NONE OR DK, Q.514a

DO NOT ALLOW REF/NULL

FOR EACH UP TO 3 CHANGES ASK Q.508a–e

Q.508b   Thinking about the most recent change, can you describe what has happened?

UNEXPECTED LARGE BILL	1
CHANGED METHOD OF PAYMENT	2
STARTED DIRECT PAYMENTS FROM BENEFIT	3
STOPPED DIRECT PAYMENTS FROM BENEFIT	4
GAS CUT OFF	5
GOT INTO ARREARS	6
OTHER (SPECIFY)	7

ALLOW DK
DO NOT ALLOW NULL/REF

Q.508c   When did this change occur?
ENTER DATE #

ALLOW DK
DO NOT ALLOW REF/NULL

SHOW CARD C
Q.508d   Did you, or anyone else, tell any of the people listed on this card about this change?
IF YES: Who was told?
CODE ALL THAT APPLY

NONE	0
DEPARTMENT OF SOCIAL SECURITY (DSS)	1
EMPLOYMENT SERVICE/JOB CENTRE	2
LOCAL AUTHORITY/COUNCIL	3

ALLOW DK/REF
DO NOT ALLOW NULL

IF CODE 1 AT Q.508d

Q.508e Did the amount of Income Support you received change after you had told the DSS about this change?

YES 1
NO 2

ALLOW DK
DO NOT ALLOW REF/NULL

Q.509a Do you use gas for heating in this (house/flat/etc)?

YES 1
NO 2

Q.509b How do you pay for gas at the moment?

| BILL PAID BY DIRECT DEBIT FROM A BANK/BUILDING SOCIETY ACCOUNT | 1 – | **Q.509c** |

BILL PAID BY CASH/CHEQUE	2 –	
DEDUCTION FROM INCOME SUPPORT	3 –	**Q.509e**
PRE-PAYMENT METER	4 –	
BUDGET SCHEME	5	
OTHER (SPECIFY)	8 –	

DO NOT ALLOW DK/REF/NULL

Q.509c How would you describe the effect of paying by direct debit on your budgeting for gas? **READ OUT LIST.**

VERY HELPFUL	1
QUITE HELPFUL	2
QUITE UNHELPFUL	3
VERY UNHELPFUL	4
NO EFFECT EITHER WAY	5

ALLOW DK
DO NOT ALLOW REF/NULL

NOW ASK Q.510

IF RESPONSE TO Q.509b WAS 4 (I.E. PRE-PAYMENT METER) ASK Q.509e.
REST: SKIP TO Q.509k

Q.509e   Did you choose to have a pre-payment meter or did the gas company insist on you having one?

RESPONDENT'S OWN CHOICE	1 –	**Q.509h**
GAS CO. INSISTED	2 –	**Q.509f**

DO NOT ALLOW DK/REF/NULL

Q.509f   At the time did you mind having a pre-payment meter installed?

YES, I DID MIND	1 –	**Q.509g**
NO, I DIDN'T MIND	2 –	**Q.509h**

ALLOW DK
DO NOT ALLOW REF/NULL

Q.509g   How would you have preferred to pay instead of a pre-payment meter?

BILL PAID BY DIRECT DEBIT FROM A BANK/BUILDING SOCIETY ACCOUNT	1
BILL PAID BY CASH/CHEQUE	2
DEDUCTION FROM INCOME SUPPORT	3
PRE-PAYMENT METER	4
BUDGET SCHEME	5
OTHER (SPECIFY)	8

DO NOT ALLOW DK/REF/NULL

Q.509h   What sort of pre-payment meter is it?

COIN OPERATED	1
TOKEN OPERATED	2
USES RECHARGEABLE KEY OR CARD	3

DO NOT ALLOW DK/REF/NULL

Q.509j   Does the meter payment collect for ... **READ OUT**

CURRENT GAS USE ONLY	1
CURRENT USE *AND* PAST ARREARS	2

ALLOW DK
DO NOT ALLOW REF/NULL

ASK ALL WHO USE GAS (CODE 1 AT Q.508)

Q.509k   Have you ever been in the situation of wanting to use the gas but not being able to?

YES 1 – **Q.509l**
NO 2 – **INSTRUCTION ABOVE Q.509m**

DO NOT ALLOW DK/REF/NULL

Q.509l   Can you tell me the reason you couldn't use the gas?

NOT ENOUGH MONEY (FOR METER/ TOKENS/KEY/CARD)	1
PLACE TO RECHARGE KEY/CARD NOT OPEN	2
PLACE TO RECHARGE KEY/CARD TOO FAR AWAY	3

CUT OFF FOR REPAIRS	4
CUT OFF FOR NON-PAYMENT	5
OTHER (SPECIFY)	8

INTERVIEWER: IF RESPONSE TO Q.509h WAS 2 OR 3, ASK Q.509m
REST: ASK Q.509p

Q.509m How far away is the place where you (buy tokens/recharge key or card)?
ENTER NUMBER OF MILES 0 – 50
IF LESS THAN 1 MILE ENTER 0

ALLOW DK

DO NOT ALLOW REF/NULL

Q.509n How long does it usually take to get there?
ENTER NUMBER OF HOURS AND MINUTES UP TO 3 HOURS

ALLOW DK

DO NOT ALLOW REF/NULL

Q.509p Thinking about the month of January 1993, on how many days did (you have no money or tokens/had your key or card run out)?

ENTER NUMBER OF DAYS 0 – 31

ALLOW DK
DO NOT ALLOW REF/NULL

Q.903c In general how well do you feel you are managing your money? Are you ... **READ OUT LIST**

HAVING NO PROBLEMS	1
JUST GETTING BY/DOING OK	2
GETTING INTO DIFFICULTIES	3
ALREADY IN DIFFICULTIES	4
OTHER (SPECIFY)	8

ALLOW DK
DO NOT ALLOW REF/NULL

ASK ALL

Q.903h Do you have a bank or building society account?

YES 1
NO 2

ALLOW REF
DO NOT ALLOW DK/NULL

Appendix 6 Secondary Analysis of the PSI Survey of Credit and Debt

This appendix describes the analysis of the information on recipients of Income Support included in the PSI study of credit and debt. The data is described in Appendix Two. In this analysis we describe the use of direct payments and deductions and compare the attitudes to debt of those with deductions and those without.

Nineteen per cent of those on Income Support had direct payments from benefit, closely matching the proportion in the ASE. Those who were divorced and those who had children were more likely to have direct payments. For example, 25 per cent of divorced people had direct payments compared with 18 per cent of those in other marital status groups and an even lower proportion (10 per cent) of widows and widowers. Among respondents with children, 21 per cent had deductions from benefit compared with 15 per cent of those without children. In the ASE lone parents were the most likely group to have direct payments. Similarly, the proportions with different numbers of direct payments corresponds to those in the ASE given in Table 2.11 of Chapter Two.

Among those with direct payments in the PSI study in 1989, 37 per cent had a payment for electricity; 37 per cent for rent; 31 per cent for gas; and 18 per cent Community Charge. As we saw at the beginning of Chapter 2, payments for the Community Charge and mortgage interest have increased since then. This difference between the types of payments made then and now should be borne in mind when considering the implications of the results of this survey.

Electricity was thus the most common payment and those with direct payments had higher expenditure on electricity than those without. Given that those with direct payments are more likely to have children and live in larger households than couples and single people, this is not surprising. It provides no evidence that people with direct payments use more fuel than others on Income Support. Expenditure on gas was no greater for those with direct payments than for those without.

Questions were asked about methods of payment for telephone and television, in addition to gas and electricity. Among those with direct payments, 88 per cent of the 23 with a telephone pay by quarterly account. Otherwise those with direct payments generally made weekly or fortnightly payments rather than pay quarterly accounts. Of the 19 with television 32 per cent of those with direct payments pay by coin meter compared with 9 per cent of those without. Those with direct payments are twice as likely to pay electricity weekly and are more likely to pay gas weekly or fortnightly than those without.

Not surprisingly those with a direct payment are much more likely to have been in arrears over the past year than those without direct payments: 79 per cent of those with direct payments had been in arrears compared 42 per cent of those without any direct payments. This compares with 49 per cent of all on Income Support and 19 per cent of the whole sample (Berthoud and Kempson, Table 8.1). However, a proportion of those with direct payments had no arrears as seen in Table 1.

Table 1 Proportion of those with and without direct payments in arrears over the past year

Number of arrears	Percentage of those with direct payments	Percentage of those without direct payments
0	21	58
1	24	20
2	19	9
3	16	5
4 or more	19	8

In some cases these arrears were not a problem but nearly half of those with a direct payment (47 per cent) have three or more debts which had been a worry or problem to the respondent.

The association between direct payments and debt is also borne out in Table 2 which shows that those who felt they were managing well were less likely to have direct payments than those who were 'just getting by' or 'getting into difficulties'. Among those who felt they are managing well, 8 per cent had direct payments, but 14 per cent of those who were just managing and 32 per cent of those who were getting into difficulties had them.

Table 2 Proportion with direct payments and feelings about managing the budget

	Manages well	Just getting by	Getting into difficulties	All
	%	%	%	%
With direct payment	8	14	32	62
No direct payment	92	86	68	262
N	**24**	**202**	**96**	**324**

A question was asked about where people would go for advice about debt. Of the 62 people with direct payments, 27 had sought advice on debt and 13 had asked the DSS for advice. Although the numbers are small, people were most likely to ask the DSS about fuel and rent debt. The main method of help offered by the DSS, not surprisingly, was a direct payment, although one respondent said that the DSS 'took everything away and sorted it out.' Seven people reported that they had no help from the DSS. The reasons they gave were: (in 2 cases) the DSS contact with the creditors was not useful; (in 2 cases) the DSS said it was the respondent's problem; (in 2 cases) the DSS gave no constructive advice; and (in 1 case) the respondent was told to sort it out with the creditor.

Analysis of this survey provided some interesting results linking use of direct payments with budgeting strategies and attitudes to credit and debt. For example, 85 per cent of those with direct payments compared with 64 per cent of those without thought debt was common. Table 3 shows that those who described their attitude to budgeting in terms of 'if the money is there it just goes' were more likely to have direct payments (26 per cent) than those who identified themselves as 'trying to keep something for emergencies'(10 per cent).

Table 3 Proportion of those with different budgeting strategies with direct payments

	Percentage with direct payments	N
If money is there it just goes	26	149
Try to keep something for emergencies	10	289

The survey investigated what respondents thought were the reasons people got into debt – was it because of not having enough to live on, poor money management or were debtors dishonest? Not surprisingly, those on direct payments were more likely to agree with the statement 'most debtors do not have enough to live on' than those not on direct payments (78 per cent compared with 50 per cent). Conversely they were less likely to agree that 'most debtors don't manage their money sensibly' than those not on direct payments (19 per cent compared with 28 per cent). Neither group thought that debtors were dishonest.

Those without direct payments had a different attitude to credit, however. They were more likely to think that credit encourages you to buy things you don't really need and that there should be tighter controls on credit.

This analysis of the PSI survey has provided some useful additional material to that available from the ASE and the SPRU survey. Although the numbers of people with direct payment and the types of payment have increased since the PSI study, the link between direct payments and debt and attitudes to managing money is unlikely to have changed.

References

Berthoud, R. and Kempson, E. (1992) *Credit and Debt: The PSI Report*, London: Policy Studies Institute.

Birmingham Settlement, Community Energy Research and the Bristol Energy Centre (1993) *The Hidden Disconnected*, Birmingham: Birmingham Settlement.

Bradshaw, J. and Millar, J. (1991) *Lone Parents in the United Kingdom*, London: HMSO.

Brady, T. and Hutton, S. (1993) *An Investigation into the Provision of Energy Advice within the Home Energy Efficiency Scheme*, Energy Action Grants Agency.

Council for Mortgage Lenders (1993) *Direct Payments for Mortgage Interest*, internal document.

DSS (1992) *The Government's Expenditure Plans 1992–3 to 1994–5*, London: Department of Social Security/HMSO.

DSS (1993) *Income Support – 1992 Annual Statistical Enquiry*, Press Release 93/96, 24 May 1993.

Ford, I. (1992) *Equitable Distribution of Payments from Income Support*, paper for PUAF, available from Ian Ford, Manchester City Council Welfare Rights Services, Central District Team Social Services Department, 27 Bold Street, Alexandra Park Estate, Manchester, M16 8AD.

Ford, J. (1993) 'Debt casts a long shadow', *Roof*, July/August, 18–20.

Ford, J. and Wilcox, S. (1992) *Reducing Mortgage Arrears and Possessions,* York: Joseph Rowntree Foundation.

Haskey, J. (1989) 'One-parent families and their children in Great Britain: numbers and characteristics', *Population Trends*, 55, 27–33.

Hutton, S. (1984) 'Domestic fuel expenditure: an analysis of three national surveys', *Energy Economics*, January, 52–58.

Mannion, R. (1993) *Direct Payments: Review of Literature and Research*, Working Paper DSS 1023, York: Social Policy Research Unit, University of York.

Mannion, R. (1992) *Dealing with Debt: An Evaluation of Money Advice Services*, SPRU Papers, London: HMSO.

NACAB (1991) *CAB Evidence: Problems with Electricity*, NACAB submission to the Office of Electricity Regulation.

NACAB (1993a) *CAB Evidence on Direct Payments of Mortgage Interest: A Submission to the DSS and the Council of Mortgage Lenders*.

NACAB (1993b) *Make or Break? CAB Evidence on Deductions from Benefit*, NACAB E/3/93.

NACAB (1993c) *Dispossessed: CAB Evidence on Mortgage Arrears and Repossessions*, NACAB, E/2/93.

National Consumer Council (1992) *Mortgage Arrears: Services to Borrowers in Debt*, discussion document, London: National Consumer Council.

OFFER (1993) *Customer Statistics*, internal report.

OFGAS (1993) *Customer Statistics*, internal report.

OFWAT (1993) Press release, July.

Parker, G. (1990) *Getting and Spending: Credit and Debt in Britain*, London: Avebury.

PUAF (1991) *Payment Direct: The Problems that Arise when Claimants have Money Stopped out of their Benefit and Paid Directly to Water, Electricity and Gas Suppliers*, Report of the round-table discussion, London: PUAF.

Ritchie, J. (1990) *Thirty Families: Their Living Standards in Unemployment*, Department of Social Security Research Report No 1, London: HMSO.

Rowlingson, K. and Kempson, E. (1993) *Gas Debt and Disconnections*, London: Policy Studies Institute.

Sainsbury, R., Hutton, S. and Ditch, J. (1994) *Changing Circumstances and the Role of Income Support*, unpublished.

Social Security Advisery Committee (1990) *Direct Deductions and Water Charges*.

Tester, S. (1987) *Social Loans in The Netherlands,* London: Policy Studies Institute.

Other Research Reports available:

No.	Title	ISBN	Price
1.	Thirty Families: Their Living Standards in Unemployment	0 11 761683 4	£6.65
2.	Disability, Household Income & Expenditure	0 11 761755 5	£5.65
3.	Housing Benefit Review	0 11 761821 7	£16.50
4.	Social Security & Community Care: The Case of Invalid Care Allowance	0 11 761820 9	£9.70
5.	The Attendance Allowance Medical Examination: Monitoring Consumer Views	0 11 761819 5	£5.50
6.	Lone Parent Families in the UK	0 11 761868 3	£11.95
7.	Incomes In and Out of Work	0 11 761910 8	£17.20
8.	Working the Social Fund	0 11 761952 3	£9.00
9.	Evaluating the Social Fund	0 11 761953 1	£22.00
10.	Benefits Agency National Customer Survey 1991	0 11 761956 6	£16.00
11.	Customer Perceptions of Resettlement Units	0 11 761976 0	£13.75
12.	Survey of Admissions to London Resettlement Units	0 11 761977 9	£8.00
13.	Researching the Disability Working Allowance Self Assessment Form	0 11 761834 9	£7.25
14.	Child Support Unit National Client Survey 1992	0 11 762060 2	£30.00
15.	Implementation of Council Tax Benefit	0 11 762061 0	£5.65
16.	Contributions Agency Customer Satisfaction Survey 1992	0 11 762064 5	£18.00
17.	Employers' Choice of Pension Schemes: Report of a Qualitative Study	0 11 762073 4	£5.00
18.	GPs and IVB: A Qualitative Study of the Role of GPs in the Award of Invalidity Benefit	0 11 762077 7	£12.00
19.	Invalidity Benefit: A Survey of Recipients	0 11 762087 4	£10.75
20.	Invalidity Benefit: A Longitudinal Survey of New Recipients	0 11 762088 2	£19.95
21.	Support for Children: A Comparison of Arrangements in Fifteen Countries	0 11 762089 0	£22.95
22.	Pension Choices: A Survey on Personal Pensions in Comparison with Other Pension Options	0 11 762091 2	£18.95
23.	Crossing National Frontiers: An Examination of the Arrangements for Exporting Social Security Benefits in 12 OECD Countries	0 11 762101 3	£17.75
25.	Lone Parents and Work	0 11 762148 x	£12.95
26.	The Effects of Benefit on Housing Decisions	0 11 762157 9	£18.50
27.	Making a Claim for Disability Benefits	0 11 762162 5	£12.95
28.	Contributions Agency Customer Satisfaction Survey 1993	0 11 762220 6	£20.00
29.	Child Support Agency National Client Satisfaction Survey 1993	0 11 762224 9	£33.00
30.	Lone Mothers: Coping with the Consequences of Separation	0 11 762228 1	£16.75
31.	Educating Employers	0 11 762249 4	£8.50
32.	Employees and Family Credit	0 11 762272 9	Forthcoming
34.	Income and Living Standards of Older People	0 11 762299 0	Forthcoming
	Social Security Research Yearbook 1990–91	0 11 761747 4	£8.00
	Social Security Research Yearbook 1991–92	0 11 761833 0	£12.00
	Social Security Research Yearbook 1992–93	0 11 762150 1	£13.75
	Social Security Research Yearbook 1993–94	0 11 762302 4	Forthcoming

Further information regarding the content of the above may be obtained from:

Department of Social Security
Attn. Keith Watson
Social Research Branch
Analytical Services Division 5
10th Floor, Adelphi
1–11 John Adam Street
London WC2N 6HT

Telephone: 0171 962 8557

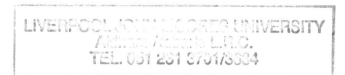

LIVERPOOL JOHN MOORES UNIVERSITY
Aldham Robarts L.R.C.
TEL. 051 231 3701/3634

Printed in the United Kingdom for HMSO
Dd300204 12/94 C7 G3397 10170